LET ME PLAY

HUMAN HORIZONS SERIES

LET ME PLAY

by

Dorothy M. Jeffree, Roy McConkey,
Simon Hewson

A CONDOR BOOK
SOUVENIR PRESS (E&A) LTD

ACKNOWLEDGEMENTS

Many of the games in the book were developed in the context of the authors' Parental Involvement Project, which was financed jointly by the Department of Health & Social Security and the Department of Education & Science. The project was based at the Hester Adrian Research Centre, University of Manchester.

We would like to thank the many parents and colleagues who gave us their comments on the book. Also Rosemary Fulton and Betty Carrington for typing the manuscript.

CONTENTS

PREFACE

Play is very important to all children's development. Through it they can acquire and master new skills. Thus with the handicapped or 'slow' child, it is vital to encourage their play. *Let Me Play* has been written especially with these children in mind, although it should be of use with any child. The main emphasis of the book is on encouraging the child's play, thereby helping him to acquire new skills. Many of the activities are linked to *specific* skills; so that the link between play and skill development is constantly emphasised.

This book is primarily written for parents. They are in an ideal position to encourage play and yet often they are unsure as to how best to do it. We aim to guide parents to appropriate activities which they can use with their child. Of course the book should also prove useful to teachers, nursery assistants and playgroup leaders.

In the Introduction, we stress the importance of play, describe how it changes as the child develops and give parents a detailed guide as to how they can encourage their child's play. The remainder of the book is divided into six sections, each one devoted to a different kind of play, e.g. imaginative play, social play. Within each section the same pattern is followed. First, we describe the kind of play the section is all about. Second, we outline the particular importance of this play in a child's development. Third, we guide parents to appropriate games and activities, given the child's present level of development. These are arranged into booklets, so that the parent can go straight to the most suitable activities. There is a wide variety of activities described within each booklet. Often these will be based on very common toys, although in many cases, we do describe special 'toys' which parents can easily make.

However, one area that is not included in this book is language development. Play activities specifically concerned with helping a child's language development are described in another book of the series, *Let Me Speak*.

Many of the games and activities in *Let Me Play* have been developed in the context of our Parental Involvement Project. But we cannot take all the credit for the ideas in the book. Many of them have come from parents and colleagues, but our main source of inspiration has been the children themselves. Often their reactions to what we thought was a good play activity have caused us to think again. No doubt, you will experience this too. We hope you and your child enjoy the games – have fun!

Since the publication of this book there have been changes in attitude towards mental handicap.

Firstly an attempt has been made to avoid *labelling* people. When this book first appeared we still spoke of 'mentally handicapped children', for instance. We now prefer to describe them as children with severe learning disabilities. The reader should bear this in mind when coming across the old terminology.

Secondly There has been a move towards the integration of children with learning disabilities into mainstream education. This widens the readership of the book. Play is vital to all children and should be shared by all alike.

INTRODUCING PLAY

The Nature of Play

Play is universal. Not only do children everywhere play, but also the young of most of the higher animals.

What then, is the nature of play which distinguishes it from other activities?

Watching children at play, one is struck by its essential joyousness. It is always pleasurable, and although at times quite serious and prolonged, it can as quickly change into a light-hearted romp.

The essence of play is that it is initiated by the child himself; it is he who chooses what to play and how to play. For, unlike work, play is carried out for its own sake, not for the sake of an end product or any reward. The act of playing is its own reward. In play a child is free from restraints and he can please himself. He can experiment without the risk of failure, because he makes his own rules.

Play is also a safety valve which prevents the build-up of frustration. Indeed we often talk of children 'letting off steam' in play.

In play, a child seems to re-charge his batteries and find fresh energy.

The Importance of Play

A kitten springing after a ball of wool, or a child bouncing a ball against a wall, is playing for sheer enjoyment. For him the game is the thing, not the good it is doing him. However, play is important, both for the growing animal and the child, for through it they are practising old skills and developing new ones.

In pouncing and springing a kitten is learning to react quickly to moving objects. This will be vital to him, if he is to catch his own food as a full-grown cat.

Similarly, in bouncing a ball against the wall a child is learning hand and eye skills, which are vital to his independence later on, for example in dressing and feeding himself.

However, an animal needs only a short period of play before he settles down into a staid adult. He has just enough time to learn those skills essential for adult life.

A human being has a great many more skills to learn, and so his childhood (or time for play) is prolonged so that through play he can acquire these skills.

How Play develops

A baby is not born able to play. This ability develops gradually, at his mother's side at first. A parent's love, and the security it brings, gives a child the courage to leave her for a time and explore his own toys – knowing she will be there when needed.

Not only this, but it is the parent who gives the child his first idea of how to play. He may discover for himself how to bang his rattle playfully, but his most intriguing toy in the early days is his own mother, who, by following his lead at first, and then letting him follow hers, encourages him to develop his play. His first game of pat-a-cake will be a direct imitation of the grown-ups. Later he will add his own playful variations. Soon his play blossoms in lots of different ways.

The Diversity of Play

There are a great many different kinds of play. For instance, play can be energetic and rough and tumble or can require great concentration and skill, like tiddly winks. Other games have an element of make-believe and imagination.

Some games require several people to play them while others can be played alone.

In each of these different kinds of play a child is practising and learning a diversity of skills. For instance, some games encourage co-operation, others help language development and so on.

Play and the Handicapped Child

Play is essential for every child's healthy all-round development. It is even more essential for a handicapped child.

However, although many children do play spontaneously without our help, this is not always true of a handicapped child. Sometimes these children are too good and seem content to lie in their cots or sit still for long periods. Other handicapped children rush around and do not pause long enough to learn to play with anything.

Parents of these children need all their skill and artistry in order to encourage their child's play. It is important that they should do so, for through play the foundations are laid for future learning. It will also mean that the child will become more active and less passive, he can start deciding for himself what he wants to do. It will widen his interests and in so doing will literally broaden his mind!

A Guide to Parents in Encouraging Play

Play must be at the right level. In order to be able to start children playing with toys it is essential to introduce games at the right level. A child will be put off by games which are either too easy or too hard for him. Observing your child will help you gauge his present level of play.

Later in the book there are developmental charts which will help to guide your observations.

Small steps – You *can* help your child's play to develop, but you must be patient. A handicapped child can only take a small step at a time. Remember, toys which seem similar to you are often at very different levels of difficulty for your child. Because your child can manage one posting box for instance, this does not necessarily mean he can manage another one, which may be much harder.

Do it again – Before moving on to another level, your

child needs plenty of opportunities to play each game over and over again. The better he is at the game, the more he will enjoy it.

Model your child's play – The best way to encourage your child's play is to get down to his level and to play with his toys yourself. The more relaxed you are the better. If your child sees you enjoying a game he will often want to join in.

Do not spoil the game in your anxiety to help your child. Remember you cannot force a child to play. He must do it because he wants to. However, you can encourage purposeful play. Show your child your pleasure in his play. Take your cue from him so that he will like playing with you and then you can gradually introduce new ideas and levels of play.

Setting the scene – Parents must be opportunists and note their child's passing interests. If he becomes obsessed with football, then is the time to buy a model football for him. Give his teddybear a scarf in the team's colours and so on. Sometimes arrange a new collection of toys when he is out of the way and let him *discover* them himself. Waning interest in old toys can often be revived if you wrap them up in paper and place them in a box. As your child unwraps his toys, each one becomes a new discovery.

If you have time, repaint faded toys while your child is asleep, or give the dolls and teddies an uplift with new clothes or shoes etc. Simple toys, made by you, often mean more to a child than expensive shop toys.

Special toys – It is a good idea to keep a few toys as a special treat. Dress up the occasion and make it a time when you can give your child your undivided attention (perhaps in the bedroom). This is especially useful if you want to teach your child a new game; a form-board or posting game, for instance. Do not let him 'mess about' with these special toys. If he does so, pack them away at once. Once your child has learnt how to play 'properly' with these toys they can be put into his 'general' play box and new 'special toys' introduced.

A little at a time – Do not expect your child to concentrate on one game for long. If you are introducing a new game, play it for a few minutes at a time and leave off *before* your child gets bored. In this way he will look forward to the next session.

He won't play with anything else – Some children seem to get obsessed with one particular toy or game and cannot be persuaded to play with anything else. Do not get too anxious about this, but try to introduce slight variations gradually.

Your child is destructive – This may mean that he is still very immature. Leave him toys which he cannot spoil and do not scold him for treating them roughly. It is best to ignore this as much as possible. Let him play with some 'special toys' with you as a treat. Make a *big* fuss of him if he plays properly. If he starts destroying these toys, do not scold him, but pack them away at once, and stop playing with him for a few minutes. Bring the toys out again when he seems ready to co-operate.

Playing alone – Do not feel you have always to be playing with your child. You will find that gradually he will be able to amuse himself and that is what you are aiming for. So give him the opportunity to get on with it.

Using the Book
We have divided the remainder of the book into six sections. Each section deals with a particular type of play. These are:
  Section 1: *Exploratory Play*
  Section 2: *Energetic Play*
  Section 3: *Skilful Play*
  Section 4: *Social Play*
  Section 5: *Imaginative Play*
  Section 6: *Puzzle-it-out Play*

Although we have divided play up into six different types, there is a great deal of overlap among the sections. The same play activity can often be classed as energetic, social and imaginative play. In some ways, it is very artificial to divide play like this. However, our main reason for doing so is to focus attention on the relationship between play and the development of particular skills, e.g. a child's physical development can be enhanced through 'energetic' play activities.

Within each section of the book the same pattern is followed. First, we describe what the play is like. Second, we explain its importance both in children's development and for the handicapped child in particular. Third, we give you an indication of which activities will be most suited to your child. Lastly, we describe a wide variety of games and activities you could use with your child.

The games and activities have been sub-divided into booklets so that you can leave out activities which may be too easy or too hard and go straight to the most suitable ones for your child.

In all six sections there is a wide range of activities, including very simple activities designed for the very young baby or the severely handicapped, right up to more complex activities suited to a more mature child. (For a brief description of the content of the booklets, see the Contents page.)

There is no need to read through the whole book all at once. You might like to use the following approach:

1. Read the Introductions to all of the sections to get an idea of the different types of play. This will help you to decide which section or sections will be particularly useful for you. You may find that your child is much better at one type of play than another. His energetic play may be more advanced than his imaginative play, for instance. You can then introduce imaginative games to help his play where it is weakest and so improve his all-round development.

2. Now go back to the sections you feel will be most useful and read through the booklets describing the games and activities. Try some of these with your child. His reactions will help to confirm whether they are suitable or not.

3. Remember these are just ideas. You may need to adapt the games to suit your child. Indeed, go on and try out your own ideas. Nobody knows your child better than you, so your ideas are well worth trying.

Sharing Ideas

However, we would like to make two suggestions, which we feel would help you to get more out of the book:

1.   *Contact other parents* – In our experience, parents can learn a lot from other parents, especially those whose children are experiencing, or have experienced, the same problems. If possible, try to contact some parents in your area – put up a notice at the local clinic or hospital; contact voluntary societies organised by parents (see Telephone Directory) or ask at your child's nursery or school or contact your Health Visitor to see if she knows of anyone.

If a group of you can get together this will give you a chance to pick each other's brains for ideas or share useful toys, books, etc. Most of all, though, you will probably find the group a source of encouragement. There will be times when you feel you are getting nowhere, but if you can talk to somebody then it won't seem as hopeless as you thought. Equally, there will be times when other people could do with your help.

2.   *Ask advice* – don't be afraid of asking for advice from professionals who are in contact with your child – psychologists, teachers, speech therapists etc. Tell them about the games you are using and if you encounter any problems or if you are unsure of what to do, then ask them if they have any suggestions. Indeed, we believe that the closer parents and professionals work together, then the more the child benefits.

SECTION 1: EXPLORATORY PLAY

INTRODUCTION TO EXPLORATORY PLAY

Do you remember wondering, as a child, what you might find in the attic or the garden shed? When you returned from your exploring with a torn pullover and dirty knees you may not have got a hero's welcome from your mother. But the discoveries you made that day probably made it all worthwhile. And when your mother's scolding had subsided, you most likely decided to go exploring again another day because your new discoveries had made you even more curious about what else you might find. This is the essence of all exploratory activity, the curiosity to find out something new. It is essential to the way we learn about our environment. In children it is fundamental to their development.

Exploration
Exploration is vital to every child's development in four different ways:
1.   *Exploration enables children to make new discoveries –* When you compare a new-born baby with a fully grown adult you realise that the baby has a lot to learn. He has to find out about himself, about the world around him and how to cope with that world. He would not learn very much, however, if he lay in his cot all day looking at the ceiling. It is through exploring his surroundings that he discovers that his world is full of different colours, shapes, sizes, smells, and so on. The more the child explores his world, the more discoveries he makes. Exploration thus helps the child to learn more about the world he lives in.

2.   *Exploration stimulates the child's curiosity* – Exploration is not simply a matter of finding out new things. By discovering that his world is full of different things a child also wonders why they are different. Why is it that my bean bag doesn't bounce but my ball does? Exploration thus not only enables the child to learn about his world but it motivates him to want to learn more. This is vitally important, for the child learns most when he wants to learn.

3.   *Exploration helps the child to develop his skills* – When a child is exploring he is not simply being curious but he is also practising many of the skills he has learned. The young baby who explores his elder sister's toy box is not merely finding out what's inside. He is developing his ability to crawl, to support himself, to reach for and to grasp objects, and maybe to throw them all over the place! Exploration thus enables a child to improve his skills and to try them out in new situations.

4.   *Exploration encourages the child to learn new skills* – As he explores his world more and more, a child learns that there are many things that at first he cannot do. The young baby crawling round the bedroom may notice his teddybear on the bed. He cannot as yet reach it but he will now be all the more eager to learn how to climb up and get it.

Exploratory Play and the Handicapped Child
We will all have noticed that most children are irrepressible explorers. Their natural curiosity is always getting them into new places and new situations, which only seem to make them even more curious and even more keen to explore. However, this may not be the case with a handicapped child. Some handicapped children, perhaps through physical impairment, simply cannot move around by themselves. They are doomed to stay where we put them, and so their opportunities for exploration can be severely limited. Other handicapped children, for example Down's Syndrome babies, are often quite happy to lie peacefully in their cots or prams. As they do not seem to demand constant attention, we tend to think

of them as 'good' babies, who give us little trouble, and so we leave them be.

This is the worst thing we can do for them because we are denying them any chance of exploring their environment. Hence we are minimising their opportunities for learning and for developing their skills and abilities.

Perhaps the greatest help we can give to a handicapped child is to encourage him to want to learn more about himself, about other people and about the world he lives in. We can do this by encouraging his exploratory play.

Encouraging Exploratory Play
How can you encourage your child's exploratory play?
1.   *You can show him that his world is worth exploring* – A child's exploratory play is nurtured by the variety of his experiences. You can encourage your child's exploratory play by filling his world with different objects and events.
2.   *Follow your child's lead* – Whatever we, as parents or teachers, may do to help our child's learning, we must remember that it is the child who actually does the learning. Like all of us, children learn most when their curiosity is aroused. You will encourage your child's exploratory play most of all by providing him with experiences which are related to his present interests.
3.   *You can show him how to explore* – Children are not born with the skills necessary for exploring their world. These skills have to be developed and you can do much to encourage this. In a sense, all the later sections in this book are concerned with helping your child to learn new skills in order that he will be better able to understand his world. Exploration and understanding are constant themes in this book and you should use the later sections in conjunction with this one.

Choosing Play Activities
In this section we describe activities designed to help your child learn basic exploratory skills which are necessary before

he learns the skills which are dealt with in later chapters. We have grouped the play activities into three booklets.

Booklet 1, *First Impressions*, suggests activities which are most appropriate for the very young baby, or severely handicapped child, who as yet cannot move around or use his hands.

Booklet 2, *Busy Hands*, describes games designed to encourage the exploratory play of children who have learned to use their hands.

Booklet 3, *Getting Around*, is concerned with exploratory activities for children who can move themselves about, even by crawling. This final section also provides further advice on encouraging exploratory play in conjunction with the other kinds of play which are described in later chapters.

You should first read the booklet which seems most suited to your child and try some of the activities with him. Note carefully your child's reaction. If he makes no attempt to join in, then you could be expecting too much of him. Try some 'simpler' activities. On the other hand, if he joins in readily but soon stops, it could be that the game is too easy and he is bored. Try some more 'advanced' activities.

It is important to choose toys and activities at the right level for your child, and this is not easy. Even the professionals sometimes make mistakes. An older child may only have reached a simple level of play which makes toys intended for his age group quite unsuitable. It is only by *starting* at the child's own level that we can encourage progress.

You may wonder how to gauge exactly what his level is. Here we can help you: as they develop, the majority of children pass through the same series of stages in learning to explore and they pass through them in the same order.

Watch your child when you give him a toy and see whether he can only cope with one toy at a time, looking at it, mouthing it, banging it or rubbing it, or whether he is starting to relate toys together by banging one with another or putting toys *into* containers or piling them on top of one another.

Be guided in your choice of activities by what you see.

A Solid Foundation

We should emphasise that a child will be most keen to explore from a basis of security and confidence. This will come from the reassurance of familiarity with his surroundings, and, most importantly, from yourself.

There are two important implications here:

1.   Before a child will be keen to explore anything else he needs to get to know you thoroughly. We suggest ways in which you can enhance your relationship with your child in *Social Play, Booklet 1: Play With Me* (p. 147).

2.   When you try to move your child on to exploring other parts of his world, your very presence will be an encouragement to him. Please don't leave him alone and expect so-called educational toys to do the job for you. For all children, parents literally have to play their part.

BOOKLET 1: FIRST IMPRESSIONS

Bonding

Probably the most important factor in any child's development is the close bond which may start to develop almost
from birth between a mother (or father) and their baby.
Nothing can replace this, and no outsider can give you a
prescription on how this bond can be cemented, since it is
such a private and individual affair, depending on the kind of
person you are and the developing personality of your baby
or child.

Sometimes it is serious, but often it is playful. These playful routines can be initiated by the infant or child himself or
initiated by you. Whatever they are, whether tummy tickling,
blowing raspberries, smiling, grimacing, baby talk, hiding
games or peek-a-boo, they are seldom published abroad.
They are something between you and your child.

Always remember that *you* know your own child better
than anyone else. Also, without the close relationship which
comes from constant handling and caressing, from boisterous
rough and tumble and from shared communication, your
child cannot develop to his full potential. It is you and your
family who are building the foundation of emotional nourishment upon which all the later ideas in this book will
family who are building the foundation of emotional nourishment upon which all the later ideas in this book will depend.

By your daily contact with your infant or child, you get to
know how far to go and when to introduce novelty into an
old routine. It is you who can best read the signs of disquiet
or fear before they have had a chance to develop further. You
also know, as we do, that with many babies who are slow in

their development, you have had to work harder to establish a bond of mutual understanding, and that it has taken longer. You have also had to avoid the temptation to handle your infant *less* because he was so good and placid. You have come to realise that these placid babies probably need more playful interaction to stimulate their activity, and not less. Or your baby may have been very remote and detached, and you have had to use all your ingenuity to find a way into his private world.

Alternatively, your baby may have been so hyperactive that you and your family have become distraught, and this has made bonding difficult. In this case most parents learn to be opportunists and make use of peaceful interludes when they arise.

We also know that this bond may be disrupted by frequent spells in hospital, but even then your visits can usually keep it going. Remember that first and foremost, you, as a parent, are the very elixir of life to your own child, and no one can usurp your place. Not only do you provide physical nourishment and shelter, but your relationship with him gives him spiritual nourishment, which is equally important.

In the following chapters we shall suggest ways of augmenting the playful interaction which you have already built up with your child and give you ideas of games to play with him at different stages in his development.

The games in this chapter are most suitable for the child who cannot yet move around, even by crawling, and who has not yet learned to use his hands to reach out and grasp objects. Such a child obviously can do little by himself to make new discoveries in the world around him. But you can help him make these new discoveries by, so to speak, doing his exploring for him. You can show him that his world is full of different things and events to see and hear and smell and feel. By doing so you will stimulate his curiosity and his willingness to make further discoveries by himself. In short, the object of these games in to encourage your child to become an explorer.

For games which help the child to learn more about his own body movements you should turn to our chapter on *Energetic Play*. The games and activities which we describe here are designed to encourage the child to become more aware of, and therefore more curious about, the world around him. Do not forget that you yourself are an important part of this world. A great deal follows from your frequent handling and holding of your child.

Support your Child
Your child will be most attentive to things around him when he is sitting up. Don't let him lie on his back staring at the ceiling. If he cannot support himself then you can do this for him, either with cushions, or with a sag-bag which moulds itself to your child's shape, or with a proper baby chair. Your physiotherapist will advise you about this. Whatever you do, it is very important to ensure that his head is properly supported (see p. 65, *Energetic Play*).

Look!
Even when you have to leave your child on his own, you can provide him with a variety of interesting objects to look at:
Mobiles – Most toy shops and fancy goods shops sell attractive mobiles and mobile Kits. We, of course, only tend to use mobiles for decoration, so we hang them very high up, out of the way.

Make sure that you hang your child's mobiles close enough for him to notice them. Secondly, try to hang them where the air currents are strongest – by the window, or above the fire or the heater. And on good days, when your child is outside, why not hang his mobile from a tree, or a washing line, or, if you live in a flat, the upstairs balcony?
Dangling Toys – These are ideal for the very young, or immobile child because they can be made or bought cheaply and they can be infinitely varied. They can also be dangled close to the child, which makes them easier to focus on, and they

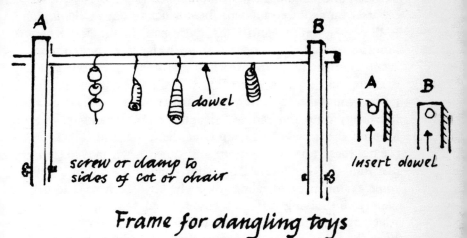

Frame for dangling toys

Fig. 1

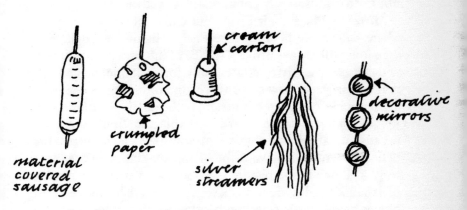

Examples of dangling toys

Fig. 2

will encourage the child to reach out, touch and eventually to grasp and handle them.

First you will need a frame from which to dangle the toys. If there is a handyman (or handywoman) in the house, get him to make a light wooden frame which can be bolted onto a cot, chair or pram (or which is free-standing if your child is sitting on the floor) – see Fig. 1. Once you have made the frame, you will need a few yards of strong elastic. Tie each toy firmly onto the end of a length of elastic, and make a loop on the other end to slip over the dowel rod. Being on elastic, these toys will bob up and down when moved, thus providing further interest for your child. Fig. 2 shows you some examples of dangling toys. The keynote here is to get variety, by having different colours and shapes, and toys which make different sounds or which move in different ways. Vary the toys frequently, dangle them in different positions, sometimes using just a few, sometimes many. You will find many suitable dangling toys around the house. If you want to buy more, some of the best and cheapest toys are found, not in toyshops, oddly enough, but in pet shops!

Mirrors – Place a mirror in your child's cot or by his chair where he can see his own face easily. His own changing expressions will always prove a source of interest. Alternatively, you can place a mirror strategically for an immobile child so that he can get a view of you moving around, or of the waving branches of the trees outside or the passing traffic.

The Thingummebob – We call this the thingummebob because it can be any shape that you like. The stranger, the better, so you will have a lot of fun making it and adding to it! The one in the picture is made out of strips, or blocks, of expanded polystyrene stuck together and then covered with bits of paper, cloth, tinsel and cotton wool. Anything will do as long as it is brightly coloured or attractive. This thingummebob fits on a short pole mounted on a wooden base (see Fig. 3). Place the thingummebob on the floor about 4 feet in front of your child, and spin it round on its base. As it spins, your child will see all the different colours as they

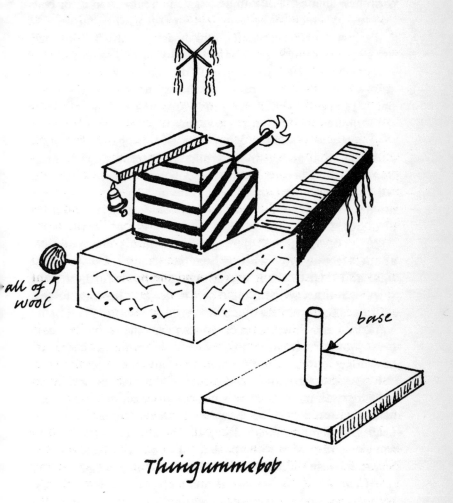

all of wool

base

Thingummebob

Fig. 3

appear. If you spin it fast enough, the colours will merge to form new shades. You can also fasten streamers to it, or bells and rattles which make interesting noises as they move.

An ingenious handyman could devise a motor for it – perhaps by mounting it on the turntable of an old record player. Alternatively, you can dangle it from the ceiling with some stout string, double-looped. You then spin the thingummebob one way and, as the string winds around itself, it will make the thingummebob spin back again.

Comings and Goings – The purpose of this game is to show your child that objects move around in space in varying directions and that he can follow these movements with his eyes. All you need is an attractive object which can be fastened to a stick (one of your child's favourite dangling toys will be ideal). Seat your child in his chair, or pram, or on the floor.

With the stick, hold the toy directly in his line of vision, about 3 feet away. Then slowly move the toy sideways to the right and then to the left, gradually moving it further to the sides each time. As your child gets better at following the toy, introduce some variety by moving the toy forwards and backwards, up and down. You could also vary the speed of movement, now slowly, now quickly (but within limits, otherwise he will get bored or not be able to follow the object at all).

It is important to extend your child's field of vision, so always try to move the toy out a little further each time. His field of vision will be increased even more if he can move his head as well. If he is not doing this spontaneously, then you can encourage him with the help of another person. As one of you moves the toy, the other turns the baby's head towards it. Of course, as you repeat this game, give him less and less help so that he can discover how to control his head by himself.

Moving objects often prove quite irresistibly attractive to young children, so be imaginative and experiment with different types of movement:

Bubbles, for example, float effortlessly in the air.

Balloons move freely and slowly and are interesting to follow without much difficulty. If you have enough helpers, then the balloon can move all over the place – even behind your child. This will set your child a puzzle as it disappears and re-appears again.

Overland – Objects that move across a firm surface travel very differently from objects moving in air, like the balloon or the toy on a stick. You can roll a ball along the floor, or bounce a ball on the floor or against the wall (even better if it rattles or squeaks); you can pull toys on a string, or you can pile up bricks and then knock them flying!

Toys on a String – You can produce a variety of movements by dragging a toy across the floor on the end of some string. Depending on the kind of toy you use (some of the dangling toys will be ideal) and the surface of the floor, you can make it slide smoothly on lino, or bobble along the carpet, hop in the air and then lie still.

Now You See It – Now You Don't! – Place a small screen on the floor three or four feet away from your child (a large book standing on its end will do). Pull your toy-on-a-string across the floor so that it passes behind the screen. Now watch your child's reaction as it re-appears on the other side!

Skittles – Young children often show great glee in watching things going flying. You can improvise a skittles game very easily with matchboxes or upright toilet-roll tubes as skittles. Send a tennis ball ploughing in amongst them or mow the whole lot down with a rolling pin!

Here I am! – Young children often delight in a game where their mother's or father's face suddenly pops up into view. Perhaps you have already played 'peep-boo' by popping up over the end of the pram or at the side of the cot. You can extend this game to encourage your child to look for you in different parts of the room.

First, you should place any handy objects – furniture, screens etc. – between you and your child. You then 'pop-up' in as many different places as possible, each time giving him plenty of praise for looking at you. Again, you may need someone else to help him look the right way initially. But don't overdo this, for the object of all these games is that your child should increase his ability to explore his world.

Here It Is! – A child's first introduction to the objects around him is made through his mother or father or siblings. You do this by showing him toys and objects and letting him feel them, and by hiding them in or under your hand and making them disappear and reappear dramatically.

What's That Noise? – In contrast to the things he sees, the sounds that a very young child hears are often of a fleeting nature, e.g. the sound of a door shutting or a car going past the house. Your child may need help in making sense of the sounds around him, otherwise he may be too confused to want to discover more about them. Therefore, while it is still important to provide your child with a wide variety of sounds, the emphasis here is to repeat these sounds frequently. In this way your child will come to understand these sounds – what they mean and where they come from. As a result, he will be even more curious when he hears a totally new sound.

You can easily include sounds in the games we have already described, e.g. dangling toys that squeak or rattle or chime. In addition, you can buy simple toys that are specially made to make sounds, such as animal noises. But don't forget that your child needs to learn about the everyday sounds in his world. These you will find all around your home – the rattle of a box of matches, the rustle of paper, water splashing in the sink, the crunch of a knife chopping carrots (but leave out the onions!).

You obviously have a wide choice, but at the beginning it would be best not to introduce too many new sounds at once. Just one or two at a time, so that your child will get to know them well. In addition, always let him see what is making the sound. In this way he will get to match the sounds he hears with the things he sees.

Mother's Voice – The first and most important sound a child learns to recognise and respond to is the human voice. Mothers learn to alter the pitch and rhythm of their voice in a playful way to gain their child's attention. Sometimes they copy his baby gurgles, sometimes they whisper or change from a squeaky to a gruff tone. Above all, they will sing to him. In this simple and enjoyable way they are laying the foundation of communication: of listening, of taking turns, and of later understanding.

Soundtrack – Here is a way of finding out how much your child has become familiar with the sounds you have been making for him. Position him so that he cannot directly see the source of the sound. When you make the sound, note whether he turns towards it. If he does so then he is obviously developing the ability to locate sounds in space.

This is an important skill and is worth further practice. You can initially give him this practice by listening to the sound of your voice. Seat your child in a chair in the middle of the room. Move around behind him to his right, then his left, sometimes high on tip-toe, sometimes low to the ground. Call to him each time you change position. With continuing practice he will become more adept at tracking the sound of your voice. But remember to keep it a game. Always reward him by coming round to his front. Let him see you and make a big fuss of him.

If your child can follow your voice successfully, you can experiment with other noises, like a squeaky toy, a whistle, the rustle of paper. Play the game in the way we have just described, but always let the child see the object *after* it has made a sound.

If, on the other hand, your child is not following the sound by turning his head or by showing signs of recognising the sound, then make the game simpler. Start with the object visible to him and then move it gradually to one side, then to the other. As he begins to track the sound, you move further round to his side and behind him. Again, make the game worth his while by bringing the object back to him regularly. (If, however, your child shows no reaction to sounds of any kind. You should have his hearing tested.)

Smell, Touch and Taste – The child who does not move or pick things up, is much less likely to exercise his senses of smell, touch and taste than his senses of seeing and hearing. He can, after all, see and hear things which may be some distance from him. But touch and taste, of course, require direct contact, and usually, to smell something, your nose needs to be quite close to it. So it is doubly important to give your child the chance to discover that his world is not only full of different sights and sounds, but of different feels, smells and tastes.

How Does That Feel? – The first experience of the sense of feel is of another human being (usually the mother) tickling, touching and caressing. It has been shown that babies who get plenty of this develop faster than those who do not, both physically and mentally. Then there is the feel of his own hands and toes and soft baby clothes. These usually come before interest in the feel of objects and toys around the house.

In your home you will have an abundance of objects and surfaces that feel different; hard and soft, rough and smooth, wet and dry, warm and cool. Where possible, let your child experience these differences as fully as possible. If the surface is large enough and the room is not too cold, take his clothes off and let him lie on the different surfaces. In the summer, of course, the garden or the park will provide a further range of surfaces and textures. However, even when your child is sitting up or lying in his cot you can let him feel a variety of materials – a hard wooden brick, coarse wool, soft velvet, a warm cup. Hold these to his cheeks, his mouth, his hands and feet.

What's That Smell? – Smells often last only for a short while (the exceptions usually being unpleasant ones!), so you must be an opportunist. Be alert to any chances that present themselves to introduce your child to new smells, such as flowers in bloom, or the smell of grass after rain. However, one regular source of interesting smells is the kitchen. So, when you are cooking, seat your child in his chair in the kitchen, near the stove if possible. As well as letting him smell what's cooking, you can explore your kitchen cupboard for the bottles of sauces, and herbs and spices. The important thing here is to get his nose right up close so he can really experience these new smells.

Taste Good? – While your child is enjoying all the smells in the kitchen, you can treat him to some tit-bits of any food which you have handy. Try him with a little piece of cheese, or bread, or cake, some salty biscuit, a slice of apple or carrot, or a spoonful of custard. He may not normally taste all these flavours, so you will be expanding his range of tastes. And even if he does have these foods regularly, they may usually be mixed up with other flavours, whereas here you are allowing him to sample the tastes separately. Keep the pieces small, though, in case you spoil his appetite for meal-time.

Hold It – You may have found that in playing some of the previous games with your child, for example, the dangling toys, he has started to reach out and grasp the toys around him. If so, then go on to the next section in this chapter, *Busy Hands*. But if your child needs further encouragement to use his hands, then here are some ideas:

Musical Mitts – Sew a little bell firmly onto the tip of each of your child's mitts or gloves. At first, use one mitt at a time. Tie the mitt onto one hand and leave the other one free. Each time your child moves his hand this will make a sound which should attract his attention. Soon he will be moving his hand *in order* to make the interesting sound, he will start to look for the source of the sound, to move his hand gently or to shake it energetically. He may explore with his other hand until he touches the bell. This is an important step forward. It is vital to encourage your child to use both hands. On another day, put the musical mitt on his other hand and leave the first hand free. On a cold day, put both mitts on at once. Start him going by taking his hand and shaking it.

You will help his activity further if you knit him a pair of mitts with different colours on each side, for example blue on the front and red on the back. He will be encouraged to turn his hand back and forth to make the different colours appear.

Jingles – Tie a string round his wrist and attach it to one of his dangling toys. Any movement of his wrist will very easily make the toy move as it is dangling on elastic.

Tickle Me – Lightly tickle his palm with your little finger so that he will close his hand round your finger. You can strengthen his grip by gently pulling against it with your little finger.

Squeeze – Put a small object, that 'gives' a little, into his palm and close his fingers round it. Place your own fingers round his and press gently, thus making him squeeze the object. This will work even better if the object makes a noise when squeezed.

See-Saw – This activity encourages the child to grip with his hands. Lie him flat on his back. Kneel astride him, take a firm hold of his hands and raise him gently into a sitting position. Then lower him down again. This see-saw action can be repeated as you sing an appropriate song ('See Saw Marjorie Daw' etc.). Incidentally, to ensure a 'soft' landing, place the inclined mat under the child (see p. 67, *Energetic Play*).

BOOKLET 2: BUSY HANDS

These games are for young children who have learned, at least to some degree, to use their hands to reach for and pick up objects. Hand skills vary a great deal in complexity. It is much easier, of course, to pick up a toy brick than it is to pick up a pin, or tie a shoelace. The development of such skills is dealt with in the section on *Skilful Play* (see p. 97). This does not mean, of course, that your child is not developing his skills whilst he is exploring or that your child is not discovering anything when he is developing his hand skills. The two are obviously very closely related and you should use the two sections together. However, the emphasis in this section is to encourage the exploration, rather than the skill, of the child who can use his hands.

Even if he is very clumsy, the child who does use his hands can explore much more than the child who does not. He can pick up the objects and toys that he sees, turn them over, pull them apart, squeeze them, put them to his mouth to taste and smell them, or shake them to make a noise. So, many of the games we described in the previous booklet will still be suitable for your child when he starts reaching and grasping. For example, he can now reach out to grasp the dangling toys himself. Through his own actions he can combine what they look like with how they feel and sound and smell.

Although your child can obviously do more for himself now, there is much that you can still do to help him make new discoveries. As we have emphasised before, variety is the essential ingredient in all his exploratory activities. You can be as imaginative as you like. Here are a few ideas:

Rummage Box – With his new-found handling ability your child will want to explore almost anything – even those things which you might think of as rubbish and would normally throw away. Instead, why not keep them in a box for him to delve into? Almost anything will do – old cotton reels, a piece of cloth, an empty sweet packet. Make sure that they are clean, as he is likely to want to explore them with his mouth. Be careful, though, not to give him Dad's Christmas cigars or his best darts!

You may find, however, that your child is most interested in the things that you handle yourselves, such as your purse or your credit cards. This is probably not because he prefers these objects as such, but because you are doing something with them. So don't just leave him to play with his own toys but join in. Give yourself ten minutes off to explore his toys with him. Do as many different things as possible with them. In this way you will encourage your child's interest in his toys and you will show him new ways of playing with them.

At this stage it does not matter whether or not he plays 'appropriately' with his toys. If he tries to bite a piece of paper, then let him. 'Appropriate' play is a matter for later chapters. For now it is most important that he be allowed, and encouraged, to discover the different properties of things around him.

Surprise Packet – You can give your child a further incentive to explore with his hands by giving him toys wrapped in newspaper or in a paper bag. Young children often take more interest in the wrappings than in the objects inside them and you may find that your child spends more time with the paper than with the toy. Alternatively, you could 'bury' a toy inside a cardboard box stuffed with wood-wool or newspaper and then let your child find it. But please keep smiling when you clear up the mess later!

Bath Time – Let your child discover what different objects do in his bath. Give him a variety, so that some of them sink, some float. Yogurt cartons can initially be floated on the water and then sunk by being filled up. Give him a plastic cup so that he can sink the cartons by pouring the water himself. In a foam bath he can make more bubbles by beating with his hands. A sponge squeezed under water will also make hundreds of bubbles. And, provided it doesn't cost nine guineas an ounce, chasing the soap under water will also prove a lot of fun!

Apart from splashing around in the bath, give him the opportunity to get the feel of other substances:

Sand Pits – Let him sit in the sand pit and wriggle his toes and plunge his hands in the sand. Yogurt cartons will be ideal for pouring sand. If you have no sand pits nearby, he can still enjoy similar experiences in the earth in your garden or in the park. Of course, if you add some water to the sand or the earth this will change their texture completely.

Dough and Clay – Both of these are soft, tacky substances which feel quite different from anything else your child will have experienced. You can buy clay in craftshops and 'Play-Doh' or plasticine in most toyshops. Alternatively, you can make your own dough simply out of flour and water, but add plenty of salt to stop it going off.

Cause and Effect – Being curious about why something happened, or what might happen, is a great spur to exploratory activity and, perhaps, to almost everything a child learns. Most of our thinking, as adults, is full of ideas of causes and effects, but this is not true of young children. Their world is initially one of bizarre, random happenings. But it is through their actions on things around them that they first develop an understanding of causes and effects. You can encourage your child's curiosity and hence his desire to explore his world, by making him more aware of causes and effects. Now that he is using his hands, you can do this very easily with games in which an action by him causes a very noticeable effect on his immediate environment. Here are some ideas:

1. *Strike!* – In a previous section we described how you can erect a toy-bar from which to dangle a variety of toys. You can also use this activity to teach the child how things move

when you strike them. If your child does not spontaneously strike out himself, then you can prompt him. Sit behind him and, holding his elbow, make his hand strike one of the objects, setting it in motion. Remember, as always, that prompting is best kept to a minimum. The purpose of this game is for the child to find out that *his* actions make the object move. If, however, he is only using one hand, then restrain this hand to prompt the use of the other one. Similarly, if he is only using one striking action, e.g. side to side, you can prompt him to hit the object back and forth as well.

2.   *Bang! Bang!* – Like the previous game the idea here is to hit an object, but this time with a wooden hammer or a drumstick. The emphasis here is to produce different sounds by striking different surfaces. If you have a toy drum or a cymbal, these are, of course, ideal but you can easily improvise with hollow boxes or tins and pan-lids. Give your child a range of surfaces to strike so that he can discover the different effects. A full coffee tin will sound very different from an empty one and a plastic plate won't clang like a pan-lid. In addition, vary the hardness of the surfaces so that he experiences different results of his banging. For example, the hammer will easily bounce off foam rubber, but not so much off wood or metal.

At first, you may need to prompt him in this game. Sit behind him and place the hammer in his hand. Then grasp his hand in yours and prompt him in hammering the different objects.

3.   *Rattling Fence* – Have you ever noticed children on their way home from school dragging a ruler across railings or a slotted fence to make a noise like a machine-gun? The handyman in the house can easily make a 'fence' as in Fig. 4 out of some lengths of wood and/or dowelling. Your child will have a lot of fun dragging a stick back and forth across his 'fence' (but not when the handyman is watching the football!).

4.   *Musical Hammering* – As a variation on the previous activity, you can teach your child to play on a toy xylophone.

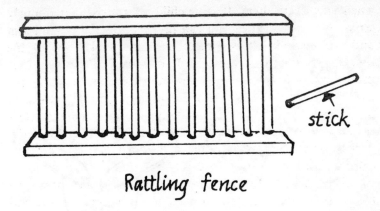

Rattling fence

Fig. 4

These are easy to play and provide the added attraction of producing various musical sounds. Alternatively you could make your own version by filling bottles with varying amounts of water to produce different notes. These bottles are best glued to a board to prevent them falling over. In one way the bottles are better than the xylophone because you can show your child, as you pour the water, how different levels produce different notes.

5. *Jumping Water Ball* – This is another game for bath time. The idea is to make a ball jump out of the water. A tennis ball is ideal here. You simply hold it to the bottom of the tub and when you let go it jumps out of the water. At first, you may have to assist your child to hold the ball under the water as it provides quite strong resistance. However, he should eventually be skilled enough to do it himself.

6. *Dancing Bears* – These toys hang on the wall and are operated by pulling the string. If you cannot buy a dancing bear in your toyshop we show you how to make one in Fig. 5.

As your child pulls the string the arms and legs rise up and as he lets go, they come down again. You can heighten the effect by tying little bells to the arms and legs. These toys are particularly useful because they help the child to learn that

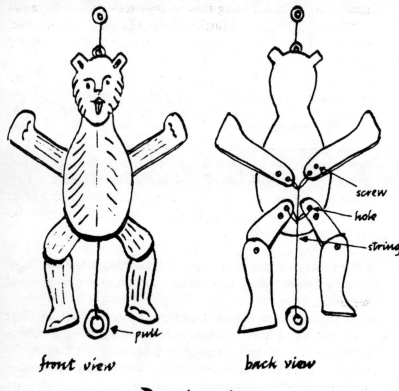

front view   back view

Dancing bear

Fig. 5

the strength of the effect is related to the strength of his own action.

You can obtain many other good cause–effect toys from toy shops, such as a jack-in-the-box or a trigger-jigger or a marble run. However, do not spend all the housekeeping on such toys because they are not an end in themselves. Their main purpose is to stimulate your child's curiosity about causes and effects. But causes and effects are also inherent in almost all the games we describe in this book. Therefore, your child's interest in causes and effects will be best maintained simply by learning how to play these different games.

When your child has further developed his ability to reach for and handle objects you can introduce more interesting games to encourage his ability to explore.

Where's It Gone? – The purpose of this game is to encourage your child to search for an object which has disappeared from view. There are many levels of difficulty in this activity, so let's start with a simple game.

Your child can reach for and pick up an object. But will he retrieve it if it's covered by another object? You can find this out by placing the object, a small ball for example, underneath an upturned glass (a strong one, mind!). Let your child retrieve it and play with it briefly. If your child cannot yet lift a glass, use a small sheet of clear polythene instead.

If he doesn't succeed in this, it probably means he needs more practice at simple reaching for and grasping objects. So give him plenty of chances to pick up the glass and the ball separately.

If, however, your child found no difficulty in finding the ball under the glass, then you have started him on searching activities which have enormous scope:

1. *Seek it here, seek it there* – Place the ball under the glass in different positions in front of the child and let him retrieve it each time. It's important, here, to give him plenty of experience in retrieving the ball from different places. If he tends only to use one hand, then restrain this hand so that he is forced to practice with the other. Eventually he will co-ordinate both hands in this game, which is, of course, a two-handed activity.

2. *Which one has it?* – Introduce more than one glass and place the ball under each one at random. If he masters this game quickly, then you can add the magician's trick of moving the glasses around after you have placed the ball under one of them. Alternatively, you could place the ball under one glass and then, before your child is allowed to reach for it, place it under another glass. These games are not as simple as they might appear for the very young or slowly-

developing child. Thus they are a good test of just how well your child has developed his searching skills.

Note that so far you have played these games with transparent covers for the object. The next level of difficulty is to use covers which your child cannot see through, e.g. small boxes, or coffee tins or even just a handkerchief. All the games which we have just described are as easily played with these covers. But remember that the covers make the game more difficult so be prepared to go back to the simpler levels of the game initially.

For the child who is visually handicapped, experiment with covers which feel different to the touch and use objects of distinctive shape and texture.

BOOKLET 3: GETTING AROUND

When your child begins to move around by himself he is really getting into business as an explorer. (For activities to encourage your child's mobility turn to our section on *Energetic Play*.) Now he can seek out new discoveries by himself without you having to bring them to him. In fact, it might seem that all you have to do now is to let him crawl or toddle around the house and the garden and the park and leave the rest to him.

It is certainly true that you have to leave it up to him in the sense that it is he who makes the discoveries. This is a fundamental point and it is well worth keeping in mind. You cannot force your child to make discoveries. But it is only part of the story.

Set the scene

Remember our point that you should make your child's exploratory play worthwhile. A bare room may not, of itself, be very interesting for him. So why not rearrange the chairs and the tables for him to crawl over or around. One or two well-placed cardboard boxes will stimulate his curiosity as to what's inside or behind them. If you leave some of his favourite toys behind them, then his exploring will become all the more worthwhile.

When your child is beginning to move around by himself, you should make every attempt to be with him when he is exploring. This will seem obvious to you because you would normally go with him to keep an eye on him. Inquisitive hands and plug points don't go well together!

But there are other very good reasons why you should be with him:

1. When children first start moving around they are often afraid to travel far from their parent's side. They will feel much happier and more adventurous in a new room, for example, when Mum or Dad is there. So, by being with your child, you are not only keeping him from harm, but you are actually helping his exploratory activity.

2. Even when your child can move around he will still need help in making new discoveries. For example, when you take him into your bedroom, open the cupboard or the drawer to let him handle your shoes or explore the different textures of the clothes. If he cannot reach them, then tip some clothes onto the bed and let him root amongst them. Sit him up on the bedroom table and let him try to touch his own reflection in the mirror. Hold him up to the window to feel the cold glass and look out over the street or the garden. This will be an entirely new viewpoint for him and you may well have to show him the view from every window in the house! Thus, even though he can move around, he still depends on you greatly to give him the opportunities to explore his fast-expanding world.

3. A handicapped child often needs extra encouragement to explore his surroundings. When you are with him you can give him this encouragement by actively joining in the exploring expedition with him. If he is crawling around the front room, then get down on your hands and knees and crawl with him. You may find, in fact, that you really are exploring because this will give you a novel angle on the world. So let your imagination run riot and enjoy it! The more you enjoy yourself the more your child will be encouraged to follow your example. Ignore all those silly remarks from the rest of the family – but be fair and make sure they all have a go!

Following on from the previous point, you may wish to

play some specific games to encourage your child's exploratory skills. Here are some ideas:

1. *Find It* – This game is a natural continuation of the 'Where's It Gone' game which we described on p. 46. Instead of hiding a toy under a coffee tin directly in front of the child, gradually move it farther away until it is on the other side of the room. You will need someone else to restrain him until you have hidden the toy. Extend the game by hiding the toy under the tin in many different places, by using more than one tin, by using natural hiding places, such as under a cushion or behind the sofa. Remember, give him plenty of praise when he finds the toy. You will find that this game will naturally expand into more than one room and, when the weather permits, you can play 'Find It' in the garden or the park. You can make more hiding places with old packing cases or with a 'caterpillar' tunnel (which can be bought at most toy suppliers listed at the end of this book).

2. *Catch Me* – As he gets better and better at seeking and finding, he may prefer to look for people rather than toys. You could start with a typical chasing game – but make sure that he is often successful himself. So don't move too fast, either when he is chasing you or you are chasing him.

3. *Hide-and-Seek* – This game can be played all round the house, or outdoors, or both. It is a game we all enjoyed as children, so we all know how to play it. However, when you introduce your child to this game, it would be best to have someone always with him, both when he is hiding and seeking, for at first, it might be a bit frightening for him to find himself left alone.

When your child eventually starts walking, he will be making new discoveries more rapidly than ever before. Not only will he be able to explore new parts of the house (by being able to reach up for things, for example) but he will also be making a 'map' of his surroundings. Because he can now move around faster he will more easily be able to work out which room is next to which, where that door leads to and what you can see outside those windows.

When he is outside he will be learning about a very new world. It will be new to him because instead of being the relatively passive spectator who was carried everywhere, he is now a much more fully-fledged member of this world because he can, literally, stand on his own two feet. Initially this new world may seem rather overpowering to him, simply because there is so much to find out in the garden and the park, the street and the shops. Obviously, like all of us, he will not be able to take in everything at once. You can best help him make new discoveries by giving him repeated opportunities to explore this new world. It may seem odd to suggest that you will help his exploring by doing the same thing repeatedly, but this is not so. When you went to the park the first time you may only have noticed the flowers or the ducks on the lake. The next time you went you may have been far more interested in the leaves on the trees, because it was autumn and they were turning brown. Thus, even when engaging in the same activities, you are still very likely to find out something new because things are constantly changing around you.

Your child is changing too and, as he develops new skills, the nature of his exploratory play will change. In later sections we describe games and activities which are designed to help your child acquire these particular skills. We would like to conclude this section not by describing any specific games to encourage your child's exploratory play, but rather by suggesting how exploratory play can be combined with the activities described in the later sections.

Many of the activities in the later sections are of a highly specific nature, with a clearly defined objective, for example, that you teach your child to hold a pencil. These activities will very often demand that, when you are working towards that objective, you do not encourage your child to do anything else. For example, if you are playing a game designed to help your child to hold a pencil, it will only hamper his learning if he starts to kick a football around the room. It is vitally important that your child should learn these various very specific skills, for they form the basis of his ability to adapt to his surroundings, to other people and simply to get more out of life. But his life is not merely a question of specific skills, nor is his learning restricted to acquiring these skills. This is where exploratory play comes in.

In exploratory play you do not have any such objective as 'holding a pencil'. Rather your only aim is that you should provide your child with the *opportunity* to explore. In this case your child may want to explore how he holds the pencil and to scribble with it. But again, he may not. You must leave the choice to him. Therefore, we suggest that you combine exploratory play with the other more specific games you may choose from the later chapters. Both types of activities will play a vital role in your child's learning and development.

SECTION 2: ENERGETIC PLAY

Introduction

INTRODUCTION TO ENERGETIC PLAY

As the title implies, this section is about play activities which require a lot of energy; activities such as climbing, jumping and ball games. The essential feature of all these activities is that often they involve the whole body. As adults we tend to think of them as 'exercising the body' and that is certainly what they do. It can be an exhausting experience joining in children's energetic play, so we hope you're fit and if you're not, you soon will be!

Yet energetic play starts long before a child learns to skip or kick a ball. Right from birth, babies engage in activities which can be considered energetic play. They wave their arms, kick their legs in the air, stretch and roll, all of which seems to be a great source of enjoyment to them. Indeed energetic play is probably the first sort of play to emerge and one that continues longest; even into adulthood, when we change its name to 'sport'! Needless to say, energetic play is very important to all children's development.

Importance of energetic play

There are three main reasons why energetic play should be encouraged, especially with handicapped children.

1. *Energetic play helps children to become active explorers of their environment* – The child who cannot move around is very dependent on adults to bring him new experiences. However, once the child is mobile, be it by crawling, shuffling along on his bottom or walking, he immediately becomes more independent. He can start to find things for himself; he can explore his world, and learn about it. The ability to crawl, walk etc.

gradually develops out of all the different energetic play activities that the baby spontaneously engages in. Thus energetic play is very important in developing the child's ability to move, which in turn, makes him more active in learning about the world around him.

2.   *Energetic play helps children to gain control of their bodies* – As adults it is hard to realise that children have to learn to control their bodies; that is, to make their arms and legs, hands and feet, move as they want them to. But watch a young child trying to kick a ball. It's obvious what he is trying to do but he just can't get his feet to do it. He may even end up falling over his own feet! Yet with practice, the control does come and this practice is energetic play. Deprive the child of this and he will find it difficult to learn to control his body.

3.   *Energetic play helps children to co-ordinate the different parts of their bodies* – This follows naturally from the above. Children have to learn to control *and* co-ordinate the different parts of their bodies so that they can work together. For example, in walking or running we have to co-ordinate the movements of our legs; shifting our balance from one to the other. The same applies when walking upstairs but here we also have to co-ordinate our arm movements, if we are holding onto the rail. Energetic play is an ideal way of helping this co-ordination between arms and legs to develop.

Energetic play and the handicapped child

We have already noted how vital energetic play is to all children's development and, of course, most children will play like this quite naturally. However, this may not be the case with some handicapped children. Children with Cerebral Palsy, because of the stiffness of their limbs, find it extremely difficult to play energetically. They will require special help and you should ask your doctor or Health Visitor (at your local clinic) to make an appointment for you to see a physiotherapist. These people are trained in helping children learn to make correct movements and often they will give you guidance as to the sort of activities you can use with your child.

When children have Down's Syndrome the problem may be the opposite in that they are too 'floppy'. With them, you again have to make a special effort to encourage energetic play, otherwise they will be content to laze in their cots!

But even if your child has none of these problems, you should still give him plenty of opportunities for energetic play.

Encouraging energetic play

Later on we will be describing activities which you can use to encourage your child's energetic play. Of course, the nature of this play changes as the child learns new things. It is important therefore to pick activities suited to your child's level of development. Otherwise he will get no pleasure or benefit out of them. So before you start any activities, it is important to find out your child's present level in energetic play. To help you to do this we have prepared developmental charts.

Developmental Charts

You should find the charts useful in three ways:

1. *The charts show the stages children go through in energetic play* – The items have been arranged in the order children usually develop them; the earliest activity is given first and the most advanced last. Thus as you read down the page, you will see the stages in the development of children's energetic play.

2. *The charts give you a framework for observing your child* – The charts highlight specific skills which you can look for in your child, or activities which you should try with him to see whether he can or cannot do them. By doing this you will learn more about your child's present level of development in play.

3. *The charts provide a means of recording your child's progress* – Beside each item you can record whether your child can (tick YES) or cannot (tick NO) do that item. If you go through the charts at regular intervals, say every six months

(marking the items with different coloured pens on each occasion), you will be able to record his progress in energetic play. This will prove a great source of encouragement to you.

We suggest that you now read through the charts. Then over the next few days observe your child and make a record of what he can and cannot do. Once you have done this, we can then guide you to suitable games and activities for your child.

Choosing Play Activities

We have grouped the energetic play activities into three booklets.

Booklet 1, *Keep Moving*, is concerned with the earliest forms of energetic play.

Booklet 2, *Finding Your Feet*, describes activities to encourage mobility, especially walking.

Booklet 3, *On The Go*, describes more advanced activities.

You will have noticed the titles of the booklets listed alongside the items in the charts. Look back at the charts; if you have ticked NO to any of the items covered by the first booklet, then we suggest you go first to Booklet 1 (p. 65) and try some of the activities given there.

If the first item you ticked NO is covered by Booklet 2, then we suggest you look at that booklet first (see p. 74) and leave out Booklet 1.

If the first item you ticked NO is covered by Booklet 3, or if you ticked all the items YES, then look at Booklet 3 (p. 83) first, and leave out Booklets 1 and 2.

Once you start the games, note carefully your child's reaction. If he makes no attempt to join in, then you could be expecting too much of him. Try some 'simpler' activities. On the other hand, if he joins in readily but soon stops, it could be that the game is too easy and he's bored. Try some more 'advanced' activities'. However, you should never try to *push* your child up to the next stage on the chart. It is often better to devise many variations on the activities he is already pract-

Energetic Play Charts

Holds head steady when supported at shoulders	YES	NO
Kicks vigorously when lying on back	YES	NO
Sits if back is supported	YES	NO
Makes vigorous splashing movements with arms in bath	YES	NO
Sits alone on the floor	YES	NO

Booklet 1 Keep Moving p. 65

Walks with help from an adult	YES	NO
Crawls on hands and knees	YES	NO
Stands alone	YES	NO
Walks alone	YES	NO
Walks pulling toy on a string	YES	NO

Booklet 2 Finding Your Feet p. 74

Kicks and throws a ball without falling over	YES	NO
Runs well	YES	NO
Jumps from bottom step of stairs, both feet together	YES	NO
Catches a large ball when thrown from 4 feet away	YES	NO
Rides a tricycle properly, i.e. steers and pedals	YES	NO

Booklet 3 On The Go p. 83

ising; this will lead to more advanced activities when the time comes. In the next section we shall give you suggestions on how to do this.

BOOKLET 1: KEEP MOVING

The activities in this booklet will probably be most suitable for a very young or severely handicapped child. *If your child is physically handicapped, make sure that you see a physiotherapist and check with her that the activities will be all right for your child.* Indeed, she will be able to suggest others which will be particularly beneficial to him.

Don't just lie there
The aim of all these activities is to encourage children to play energetically, even at an early age. However, one of the simplest ways of doing this is not through special games or using special toys, it is simply moving the child around and putting him in different places. Here are some examples:

Swinging – Being lifted by an adult and swung around can be great fun for children and it lets them experience all kinds of different movements. You can do this from an early age (babies after all are sturdy creatures, not bone china); although with an older handicapped child it can be quite exhausting. This is definitely a job for Dad. Have a short period each day to give him a good swing – from side to side or up and down; either on his back, tummy or upright.

Different Surfaces – Let your child experience what it is like to lie on different surfaces. Some can be hard and unresponsive to his movements (floor) whereas others are soft and will wrap round him (pillows, eiderdowns or a large beach ball, partly filled with air). The different feel of these materials will encourage the child's movements (see *Exploratory Play*, p. 40).

Bath Time – Water is probably the most responsive of all materials and bath time is invaluable for encouraging energetic play. Splashing and kicking are so much more fun when you can feel and see the effects you cause; not least, Mum and Dad getting soaked!

Bouncing Cradle – The disadvantage of cots and prams is that they are too sturdy to respond to the child's movements. However, with a Bouncing Cradle (available from Boots or Mothercare), as the child moves, so the cradle rocks, which in turn encourages the child to make more movements. They are, however, designed for the young baby and would not be suitable for an older handicapped child. For him you might use a hammock (obtainable from large stores) or you could make your own out of strong canvas material and nylon cord. But do make sure it is safe and that your child won't topple out of it easily. Hammocks have the same effect as the Bouncing Cradle; the child can easily make it rock back and forth, or bounce up and down in it.

Swimming – With the help of aids, even very handicapped children can have the sensation of floating in water. This is a great incentive for them to move their arms and legs. Try to take your child along regularly to the local swimming baths. Many swimming baths now have proper children's pools, which are much warmer than the main pool. This is a blessing for both you and your child, especially if you are not moving around very energetically.

Inclined Mat – It is important to have your child lying on his tummy as well as his back. This is less attractive to a child for he cannot look around so easily nor play with toys. You can overcome these problems by making an inclined mat for him to lie on. Buy a piece of *stiff* foam rubber, two foot by three foot and six inches deep (or bigger depending on the size of your child). Cut it diagonally so that it tapers, then cover with waterproof material to keep it clean (see Fig. 6).

You then lie your child on the mat with his head and arms over the side. Place some toys close by for him to handle. The mat is particularly good for getting him to move his head.

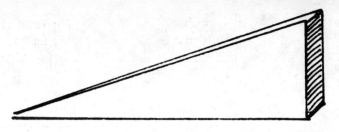

Wedge of foam
Cover with fabric

Inclined mat

Fig. 6

(This is particularly difficult if you are flat on the floor.) For example, when he is on the mat, kneel in front of him or to one side, and call his name. He will have to move his head to see you. Alternatively use a 'noisy' toy (rattle, bell etc.) to get his interest.

Sit Up – It is also important to let your child experience sitting up. At first you will have to support him yourself or with pillows, cushions etc. With a very 'floppy' child you could make a specially tailored support out of foam rubber; particularly for his head. Or use a 'sag bag' (see p. 32).

In a sitting position, the child can see many more things (so little happens on floors, still less on ceilings!) and it will be easier to handle toys, especially if you fix up a low table for him, preferably with raised edges to stop toys rolling off.

As he gains experience you can gradually reduce the amount of support so that he can develop his sense of balance.

Play Activities

Before we start describing the activities you could use, there are some general points which you should bear in mind when playing with your child:

1. *Be relaxed* – As you play, talk to him in a quiet, soothing voice. Indeed the more relaxed you are, the more confident he will be in taking part in the activities.

2. *Smooth handling* – As you move him, avoid any sudden or jerky movement. First, talk to him, let him see you, then move him in a slow and smooth manner.

3. *Don't fight against resistance* – If, when moving your child, especially his arms and legs, he fights against it, don't go on. Relax him before trying again.

4. *Encourage active movement* – In many of the activities you will be making the child do certain movements. While this will benefit him, it is even better if you can get him to make the movements by himself. This is what you should aim for, and throughout we will be suggesting ways in which you can do this.

5. *Both sides* – Make sure that you encourage movements on both sides of the body. Some children may have a distinct preference for one side and will avoid using the other. Look out for this. If it is so, then concentrate on the 'lazy' side.

6. *No clothes* – Clothes can be very restricting to a child's movement, so if your room is warm and cosy, take his clothes off and place him on a waterproof sheet or use a 'changing' mat obtainable from Mothercare or Boots. He will have much greater freedom of movement.

Now for some activities.

Rolling Over – Rolling is probably the earliest sort of energetic play for any child. It not only gives him the experience of moving but also of lying in different positions; on his tummy, side or back. At first, you will have to do it all for him. For a smooth roll from the back onto the tummy, here's what to do (see Fig. 7).

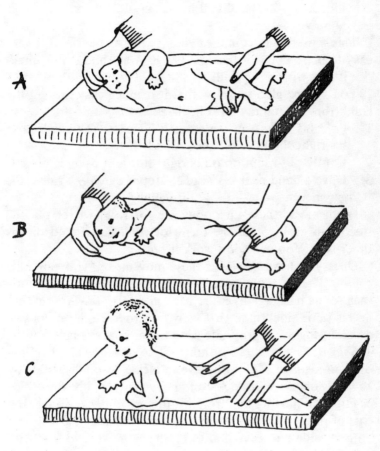

Rolling over from back to tummy

Fig. 7

1. Put your *left* hand under your child's *left* knee. Move it towards his right side and as you do, gently bend his leg. Make sure his other leg remains reasonably straight.
2. With your *right* hand, stretch our your child's right arm above his head.
3. Continue moving his leg over and let his outstretched arm slide under his head and he will gradually come onto his tummy.

This sounds very complicated but after a few tries it is very easy to master. But rather than have your child suffer, practice it first with a rag doll!

You will be glad to know that it is much easier to get the child from his tummy onto his back.

1. Fold his *right* arm underneath his chest. This will raise his right shoulder off the ground.
2. Gently push him onto his right side and over he goes!
3. Have a hand near his head to stop it banging against the ground.

(Remember, these directions are for rolling over on one side. You have to change them for rolling the child on his other side. You will soon work it out!)

Once you have mastered these movements, you can start rolling. That is, move your child from his back to his tummy, then to his back again; either back and forth (always turning on his same side) or so that he rolls across the floor. As you do this, sing an appropriate song or nursery rhyme.

Solo Rolling – Our aim though is to have the child rolling over on his own. This you have to tackle gradually. Start by having him do a little bit of movement on his own. For example, in moving him from his tummy to back, do the first part of putting his arm under his chest and start moving him onto his side but leave him to finish the movement – gravity will help!

You can use this sort of strategy with any activity. *You do most of the movement for the child but leave the last bit for him to do on his own.* Gradually have him doing more and more until eventually he can do it all by himself.

Alongside this, you should also make it worthwhile to turn over. There are lots of possibilities but here are two examples:

Seeing you: If your child is on his tummy, kneel beside him but out of sight and call him. As he rolls over (maybe with your help), he will see your face.

Noisy toy: You can do the same thing with an object which makes a noise – squeaky toy, musical toy, rattle, hand bell. If he turns over, he can have the toy. In order to maintain your child's interest in these, only let him play with them for a short time and keep them specially for these 'learning' sessions. Don't let him have them all the time.

Finally, remember to get him rolling over on both his right and left side.

Roller – This is a very valuable piece of equipment and is easily made by stuffing a specially made 'bag' with scrap material, such as wool, old tights etc. or foam pieces (see Fig. 8). Or alternatively, by wrapping 3″ thick foam rubber around a tube (e.g. cardboard tube in large tin-foil packets or plastic tubing available in hardware shops) and sticking the ends together before covering with material (preferably plastic).

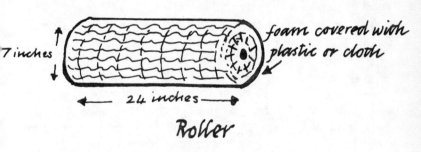

7 inches

foam covered with plastic or cloth

24 inches

Roller

Fig. 8

Here are some ways in which it can be used:

(a) As an alternative to the inclined mat, especially with bigger children (see p. 66).

(b) Place the child on his tummy with his arms over the roller and his chest lying on it. Hold the child by his thighs and gently push him so that he rolls forward. Then gently pull him back. Place an attractive looking toy just out of reach to encourage him to stretch out for it. Roll him towards it and when he has caught hold of it, pull him back.

This activity develops the child's arms and shoulder muscles, encourages him to stretch out and lets him experience moving on his tummy (preparation for crawling).

(c)　Place the child on the roller as before, only this time hold his arms and pull him forward, leaving his legs free to dangle in the air. You could encourage him to kick by placing some dangling toys over his legs (see later).

See-Saw – This activity encourages the child to grip with his hands, stretch his arms, and it will exercise his tummy muscles. Lie him flat on his back, then kneeling astride him take a firm hold of his hands and raise him gently into a sitting position. Then lower him down again. This see-saw action can be repeated as you sing an appropriate song ('See Saw Marjorie Daw' etc.). Incidentally, to ensure a 'soft' landing place the inclined mat under the child. This game is good exercise for parents too!

Stretch Out – You can continue getting the child to stretch out by placing toys close to him so that he has to reach out to get them. If he is lying down, place them all around him so that he has to stretch in lots of different directions.

Arms and Legs – In order to let the child experience lots of arm and leg movements, you can do the actions for him. Take hold of his hands, gently move his arms – in circular movement, up and down, in or out; both together, one at a time, in the same or opposite directions – there are lots of variations. Remember though, don't fight against any resistance.

Similarly you can move his legs, although these have less freedom of movement at the best of times and even less if the child wears a nappy – so remove it. Here you can move the legs in a bicycling movement or lift them up in the air, then let them fall to the ground (use a pillow for a soft landing). (As you do the actions, sing a song or nursery rhyme.)

Bash It – It is much better, though, to have the child making these movements for himself. Here is a way of doing it.

Suspend some brightly coloured toys, which make a great deal of clatter when hit (e.g. rattles, belts, teething rings), above the child. His cot is a good place for this. String cord across it and from it hang the toys, also connected by cord or fine elastic.

Position the toys so that if he moves his arms, he will hit them and cause a great clatter (definitely a day-time activity!).

Later, position them over his feet to encourage movement. As he won't be able to see the toys, you will have to move his legs for him at first, to let him find out that the toys are there.

If the child has a 'weak' side, then place the toys nearer this to encourage him to move on that side.

(For more about dangling toys see *Exploratory Play* (p. 32) and *Skilful Play* (p. 111) sections.)

BOOKLET 2: FINDING YOUR FEET

The activities in this booklet follow on directly from the last one and they are mainly concerned with helping the child to become mobile, especially through walking. This is a difficult skill to master. In order to walk, children need to have sufficient strength in their leg muscles; they must be able to control and co-ordinate their leg movements and, most importantly, be able to balance their weight on their feet. Quite a task for any child but even more difficult for the child who is handicapped.

But as with the learning of all tasks, the important thing is practice, and there are lots of different ways in which children do practice. The activities described in Booklet 1 form the foundations for walking. If your child has mastered them, then you can certainly move on to the activities described below.

The essential thing to remember in all these activities, is that children will move, be it rolling, crawling or walking, *if it's worthwhile*. Sometimes we actually *discourage* a child from moving in that we hand him the things he wants. So he doesn't need to move. (NOTE: *If your child is physically handicapped, consult your physiotherapist before starting any new activity*.)

On your feet
It is important to let the child experience taking his weight on his feet. You can do this by holding him upright and letting his feet touch the ground. Note if he straightens his legs and takes his weight while you lower him further. If he

does, count how long he keeps it up before 'collapsing'.

If he doesn't take his weight, get somebody to push his knees in so that his legs are straight and feet flat on the ground. Lower him down and see if he takes his weight now. Keep a count of how long he does so. However, this can be a back-breaking experience so it is worth using either or both of the following, but first check with a physiotherapist if your child is physically handicapped.

Baby Bouncer – These are available in the shops (e.g. Mothercare) but as they are primarily designed for young babies, you may have to make your own for the older handicapped child.

The child is simply placed upright in a canvas seat which is attached to a spring and the whole lot is suspended from a doorway. The child has considerable freedom of movement. He can bounce up and down, turn around, swing back and forwards; that is, as long as he moves his legs. To encourage him to do this, place a toy at his feet that will make a noise when he knocks against it. Only use the Bouncer for short periods of time. It is not doing him much good if he is only 'hanging' in it.

Baby Walker – Here, too, the child can experience 'standing' but as this is designed for babies it may not be suitable for the older child unless you modify it. As the name implies, the idea is to allow the child to move around through pushing with his legs. However, the main benefit is in helping to build up leg movements and strength. It will *not* encourage the child to walk, and so should be used sparingly. However, the child can be encouraged to use his baby walker as a 'push-along' toy. This will give him practice at walking (see later).

Push Off

This activity will also help to develop his leg muscles. Lie him on his back, and then kneel by his feet and place them against your chest and lean forward so that his legs bend and his knees nearly touch his chest. He will probably start resisting your movement and push against you. If he does, move slowly back. You can repeat this, going backwards and forwards. As he gets used to it, wait until he pushes harder before you move back.

Alternatively, you can place him close to a wall, so that he can experience pushing against it with his feet (with the consequence that he will move). Or with the roller (see p. 71); hold it against his feet and keep it there until he pushes it away. Both of these activities work best when your child is lying on a shiny surface.

Extended See-Saw

You can extend the See-Saw game described earlier (see p. 72) to help your child learn to stand. Now, you not only pull him into a sitting position but continue by lifting him into an upright position. Let him stand for a few seconds then back down again; first to a sitting, then to a lying position. Repeat until you tire! Singing a song or nursery rhyme will help you to keep the rhythm. You can vary the speed: sometimes fast, other times slow.

As you do this activity, you will notice your child becoming more active in the movements and you will not need to *pull* so much. Encourage this for the more active he is the better.

Crawling

The roller can be useful in encouraging the child to crawl. We have already described how it can be used to help arm and leg movements (see p. 71). An extension of these activities is to place the child with his tummy on the roller and his arms on one side, legs on the other. Move the roller slowly forwards and backwards so that the child leans alternately on his hands and feet. Gradually he will become more active in pushing himself forward – the beginnings of crawling.

Continue this, without the roller, by placing the child in the crawling position and leaving an attractive object just out of reach. This will encourage him to move forward, and as he becomes capable of doing this, move the object gradually further away so that he has further to go.

Standing

Once your child can support his own weight for a minute or so, you can start standing him against furniture – chair, settee, low table. Be ready to catch him though should he fall over. Also make sure that his feet are in the right position; you don't want to teach him any bad habits.

In this position, the child will be able to play with toys so put some on the chair. This may give him an added incentive to stand. You can get him reaching out if you move the toys to the side of him and this will give him practice at balancing.

Getting Up

Alongside these activities you should also be encouraging your child to get up on his feet by himself. At first, he will only be able to do this if he has something to lean on or to pull himself up by. Make sure you provide him with these – low stools or pouffes – as sometimes ordinary furniture can be too high for the child.

Remember that children often make an extra special effort to obtain the thing they want. If you place his favourite toy on a chair or the settee, then he will have to get on his feet to obtain it. Do this gradually though. At first, let him have the toy as soon as he makes an attempt to get up. When he is used to doing this, expect a little more from him until eventually he can get the toy by himself. And give him plenty of practice for he has a lot to learn.

Moving when Upright

Getting him moving in an upright position is literally the next step! One way of doing this is by scattering the toys on a settee so that he has to move sideways to get them. This is difficult for the child as he gives the impression of being stuck to the ground – as indeed he is. Try this strategy:

1. When the child is standing playing with a toy, move his

body gently to one side so that one leg is taking more weight than the other.

2. Move the free leg a little to one side and let him stand on both feet again.

3. Then move his body so that the leg which you moved takes the weight, which enables you to bring the other leg alongside.

In this way, the child will experience moving sideways. Encourage this by placing a toy out of reach and giving him help when necessary.

However, although this activity will help his balance and co-ordination of his leg movements, it is not really all that similar to walking. The next two activities may be more suitable.

Push-a-long Toys – There are plenty of these available on the market. Alternatively you can use a baby walker. When first using a push-a-long toy, the child may have difficulty keeping up with it – so you should control the speed of it. Do not use the toy on smooth surfaces. Carpets, lawns etc. are best. Also you may need to weight the toy in some way, e.g. if it is a 'brick carrier', put some heavy objects in the tray. This will make it harder to push but don't overdo it or your child will not be able to budge it!

Another point to note is that the bar on which the child leans should not be too low (especially for the older handicapped child). If he has to stoop, you will then need to make the bar higher by adding a piece of wood or metal to the supports.

Parallel Bars – A handyman could make these, using broom handles for the bars on a simple frame (see Fig. 9). It is less troublesome if one of the bars is attached to a wall and the other is portable. Here the child has to move both his arms and legs to make progress along the bars. Placing a ball at his feet will encourage him to move them though.

Standing Alone

Here is a good test of the child's ability to balance – can he

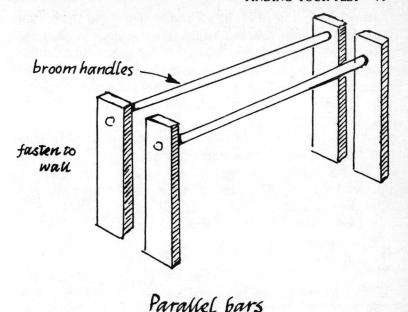

broom handles

fasten to
wall

Parallel bars

Fig. 9

stand alone? Approach this gradually though. For example, stand him against a chair and get him interested in a large toy which requires a two-hand grasp, e.g. a large 'ridged' ball (e.g. baby's first ball – obtainable in toy shops) attached to a piece of string with strong tape. Lift the ball up so that the child has to raise his hands to keep hold of it. Then have somebody slowly remove the chair so that the child has nothing but the ball to hold onto. Release the tension in the string and see how long the child remains standing.

Walking Alone
Having come this far, there is just the milestone of walking by himself. As before, this is something you should tackle gradually. Here are some ways in which you can encourage children to take at least a few steps unaided.

Catch me – Place your child at arm's length and kneel

facing him. Let go of his hands and let him stand alone. (But if need be, let him lean against the settee or chair.) Encourage him to walk towards you and when he attempts to do this cuddle him to you, before he has a chance to fall. When he has learnt to 'walk' this short distance, you can gradually move further away. If you talk or sing to him as he walks, it will keep his attention focused on you.

As an incentive to get him to walk to you, you can hold his favourite toy or some interesting object.

Push-a-long toy – If your child is used to walking with a push-a-long toy, place him against a wall or chair etc. and put the toy a little bit away but still within reach. Let him get used to reaching forward and walking with the toy. When he is used to this, move the toy a little further away so that he will have to take a step forward to get to the handle. When he has mastered this you can gradually increase the distance until he walks several steps before reaching the toy.

Parallel Bars – Similarly if your child has been using these encourage him to walk on until he reaches you. At first, position yourself very close to the bars, then *gradually* increase the distance he has to walk.

Round in circles – This game can also be useful in giving the child confidence in moving around. Arrange a circle of chairs fairly close together, with the child in the middle. The idea is for him to walk from one to the other in search of a toy or some other object which he wants. At first have the chairs close enough for him to get from one to the other while holding on. However, gradually increase the distance so that he will have to move unaided, and yet not too far or he will lose confidence. If he is to persevere at this game, then you have to use an object which he really wants.

Kicking

Kicking gives the child excellent practice in finding his feet. You can save yourself a lot of work in chasing after balls by attaching the ball to a piece of string. Cloth balls or hard plastic balls with holes in them (obtainable from sports shops) are best for this. Alternatively, a large, brightly coloured, but light beach ball will prove very responsive to the smallest kick.

If the child is sitting on the floor, place the ball at his feet and then move his leg in a kicking action to show him how the ball will move. You can then pull the ball back with the string. Encourage him to kick the ball by himself and when he does, make a great fuss.

If the child is sitting in a chair, you can dangle the ball near his feet, so that when he moves his feet he can't help but 'kick' the ball. Of course, you can use any sort of toy here (e.g. rattle); in fact the noisier it is, the better.

At the bar – Here is a way for the child to practice kicking while standing. Suspend the ball (or other toy) from one of

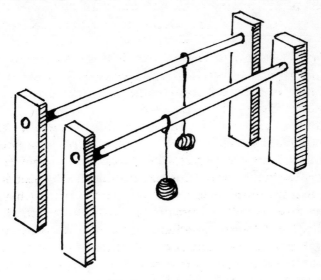

*Parallel bars
with dangling toys*

Fig. 10

the parallel bars so that it nearly touches the ground (see Fig. 10). As the child stands at the bar, he can kick the ball and as it is on string, it will always come back to him. At first he may want to handle the ball or toy but encourage him to keep standing and to kick it instead.

BOOKLET 3: ON THE GO

The activities in this part will be most suitable for children who have started to walk, although there are some which you could use with physically handicapped children who are unable to walk. We have arranged the activities in an approximate order of difficulty. The ones described first are to help the child's walking ability. These follow on from the activities described in Booklet 2 (see p. 74). The other activities are rather more advanced but as you read them you will probably know if they will be beyond your child. However, nothing beats a try; so have a go and watch how he reacts. Maybe it won't be too difficult for him after all!

Questions answered
Before we describe some games and activities we would like to answer some of the questions parents frequently ask when it comes to this sort of play; questions like:
Won't he hurt himself? With energetic play activities there is always a danger that the child might hurt himself. Obviously you have to take certain precautions and often you will be supervising him. However, this shouldn't be to the extent that you do not let him play these games just in case he hurts himself. Parents often have this attitude when it comes to climbing, especially climbing the stairs. They do not let their child try to climb on his own. You may think it is for his own good, but in reality you could be doing him real harm in that he is deprived of the opportunity to learn and his physical development may be held back.
Won't he learn bad habits? There is a risk, if you encourage

the child to play some activities, e.g. jumping or kicking, that he might start jumping on your new settee or kicking the cat! The important thing here is *not* to stop these energetic play activities but to teach when these activities are all right and when they are not. That is, what he can jump on or kick. *And when you say NO, you have to mean it.* Don't let him get away with it.

How can I get him interested in new activities? The best way we know is simply to play the game yourself, and practically ignore him. It's surprising how quickly children will start to show an interest. When they do, let them join in. However, *do not coax.*

Some points to note though: At first make the game as simple as possible. Concentrate on the essential part of the activity and when he has mastered this you can extend it. If you can get another child to play the game, all the better. Children often copy other children more than adults.

What if he doesn't like energetic activities? There certainly are children who don't like too much energetic play.

Children's dislike of energetic play may stem from a fear of falling and hurting themselves. You will then need to build up their confidence. Give them lots of help at first; hold them, be ready to catch them and if they do fall, don't make too much fuss. Reassure them but get them back into the activity as soon as you can. However, like all play activities, they should be enjoyable for the child.

You may even have discouraged energetic play, thinking it could be harmful for them. While this may be so with a small proportion of children, most children can only benefit from energetic play. It will exercise their bodies and avoid problems with digestion and obesity. Hence you should encourage energetic play unless you have medical advice to the contrary.

Here are some games and activities you could use:

Rough and Tumble – This is especially good for helping the child to balance and co-ordinate his body movements. Children love it, for they can experience all sorts of different movements; rolling over, falling down, doing somersaults etc. We are not suggesting that you do all these things straight-away. Rather you should gradually make the rough and tumble more active as your child gets used to it. Although it may be exhausting for you, a short session each day is well worthwhile.

Ride 'em Cowboy – This activity is good for developing the child's sense of balance but it can be exhausting for the parents. It's simply this: Dad is the horse and kneels on all-fours. The child is the cowboy and sits on his back with his legs apart and holds onto Dad's pullover (wear an old, loose fitting one). Dad then crawls around the room (it's hard to gallop!) while the child tries to keep sitting on his back. At first he will find it difficult to keep his balance, so take it slowly and Mum, be ready to catch him. As his balance improves, you can start speeding up and later, try as you might, you may not be able to shake him off.

Tidy Up – The idea of this game is for the child to walk around the room picking up objects and then placing them in a box. This will help to consolidate his walking skills and will give him practice at kneeling down to pick things up off the floor.

Here's what you do. Cut a hole in the side of a cardboard box and place it in the middle of the room. Scatter some of the child's toys around the room. Show your child what he has to do. Go to an object, pick it up, walk to the box and drop it in. As you do so, cheer loudly and make a great fuss. Repeat for the other objects, perhaps letting him do the drop-ping in, then later encourage him to do the whole thing by himself. Seeing the objects disappear into the hole can be in-triguing for the child, although you may have to stop him from pulling them out again!

It may take a while before he gets the idea but it's worth sticking at it; not least because he will learn to tidy up!

Dangling a Carrot – This activity is designed to encourage the child to walk. It is a variation on the old idea of getting the child to walk by offering him a toy and as he comes to get it you walk away, so that he has to walk all the more. In this game, the adult doesn't do any walking, just pulls some strings, so it is more intriguing for the child.

Here's what you do: Tie the ends of a long piece of string (25 feet or more) so that it is a continuous circle. Loop it over a door handle and then move away so that the string is tight. Attach a toy to the string (balloon is best) so that it is at or just above your child's eye level when standing (see Fig. 11).

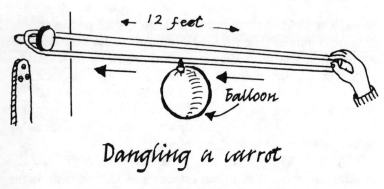

Dangling a carrot

Fig. 11

If you now pull on the string, the balloon will move along, either towards the door or to you. Encourage your child to walk along trying to get hold of it. Adjust the speed according to his ability and if he falls, stop pulling on the string.

You can also give the child practice at turning, by suddenly changing the direction so that he has to turn and go in the opposite direction.

Also you can keep his interest by using different toys, but keep them lightweight, otherwise the string sags.

Walk the Plank – This is a more advanced walking activity as it requires the child to walk within a narrow area and in a particular direction. Yet all it involves is literally walking on a strip of wood or something similar (e.g. polystyrene and bricks). Needless to say this may need to be an out-of-doors activity. A good size for the 'wood' is 8 feet long and 6 inches wide.

This can prove quite difficult for a child who is just learning to walk so at first, hold his hands, then gradually let him do more and more on his own. When he is able to do it by himself, you could make it a little more difficult. For example, by placing the strip of wood on bricks, so as to raise it off the ground. Or by placing some simple obstacles in the way, so that he has either to step over them (e.g. tin box, toy) or bend down to go under (e.g. a scarf at chest height). You can also use a narrower strip.

An even more advanced form of this activity is to use a ladder, laid flat on the ground, and the child has to walk from rung to rung.

Chasing – Chasing games are an ideal way of developing the child's running ability. You can have many variations. He has to try and catch you: maybe to get the toy or sweet you have for him. Alternatively, you can chase him, pretending you are going to take back the toy etc.

Another way is to race him to an object. A ball can be very useful here; he has to run to get it before you do or run after it if you kick it away.

These are very much outdoor games, requiring lots of room but preferably played on grass or sand to avoid bumps and grazes.

Hurry! Hurry! – This game should also encourage the child to move faster. Attach a toy to a long piece of string which is then looped over a hook in the doorway (see Fig. 12). This means that the toy can be moved up and down when the string is pulled.

Position the child some way from the toy and he has to run to get it. Start off with the toy high up and a cardboard box underneath for the toy to drop into. Gradually lower it and as you do so, your child has to run to get it before it disappears into the box. Adjust the speed at which you lower the toy to suit your child's abilities but *don't* let him get it every time. Shouts of encouragement will help or you could turn it into a race between him and Dad or Mum.

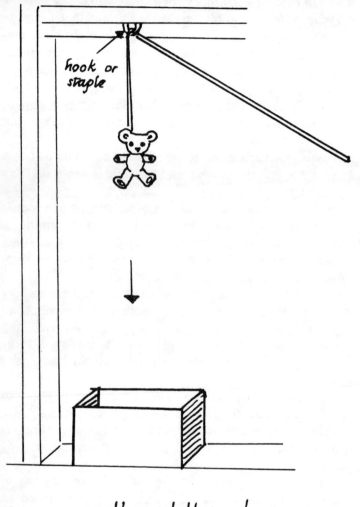

hook or
staple

Hurry! Hurry!

Fig. 12

Climbing

Once children have found their feet, climbing up onto furniture etc. soon follows. This is their way of practising balance and co-ordination and although good for them it may not be good for your furniture. Take them to a playground for climbing practice: especially slides or climbing frames. Slides are particularly good for they give children practice at climbing and the sliding down helps their balance. However, not all slides are designed with handicapped children in mind. You may need to walk up behind and be ready to catch him should he lose his balance.

You can improvise a slide at home, by placing a piece of wood (12 or 18 inches wide and 8 feet long) on the stairs and anchoring it firmly at the bottom. Wood covered in melamine or gloss paint is best.

At first, start with a gentle incline, e.g. place the top of the slide on the second stair. You can then increase the steepness by placing the top on a higher stair. As your child becomes used to sliding, encourage him to try different ways of coming down, e.g. on his back or tummy; head first or feet first etc.

Stairs

Stairs often have a natural fascination for children and you should give them an opportunity of climbing *up and down*, under your supervision, of course. At first your child will probably go up on all fours. You should gradually encourage him to walk upright. You can do this by having him hold the rail and walk upright for the *last* step. This means that he will be able to carry on walking when he gets to the top. Gradually increase the number of steps he has to take upright (two, three etc.) until he can do them all upright. Coming down stairs is much harder. If he comes down on his bottom, you can use the same idea. At first, have him stand up for the last step, then for two etc.

Having your own slide on the stairs (see above) can be a good incentive for the child to practice climbing.

Jumping

Jumping will also help to develop their balance and co-ordination. However, children can be very reluctant to take both feet off the ground; they prefer to step down or step over something, always keeping one foot on the ground.

Jumping, with both feet together, is something they have to learn to do. There are lots of ways you can encourage them.

Jumping Up and Down – Simply stand in front of him, holding his hand and encourage him to jump up and down. If you do this to music, you can 'pretend' it's dancing or alternatively suspend some toys above him so that he has to jump to grasp them.

Jumping on a small trampoline (or trampette) is very good practice for jumps are much more effective if both feet are used together. Most trampettes have a bar attached for the children to hold on to, otherwise you will need to hold their hands. You may be able to borrow a trampette from your local Toy Library (see Addresses, p. 250).

Jump Off – Encourage him to jump down, again using both feet. At first this will only be from the bottom step of the stairs or from a low stool – with you holding both his hands. As he gains more confidence, you can increase the height from which he jumps.

However, some children may need special encouragement to jump. Here are two ideas –

Squeaky cushion – You can usually get these at joke shops; although they do make rather a rude noise! Place the cushion at the bottom of the step so that when the child jumps, it squeaks!

Splash – This is very much an outdoor activity using paddling pools. Place a low stool in the pool which should have a few inches of water in it. If the child jumps off the stool with both feet, then he will make a great big splash! Remember, children can drown in a very few inches of water, so keep a close eye on them.

Jumping over – You can have your child jumping over all

sorts of things, although to reduce the risk of tripping, you should hold one end of the rope and be ready to drop it, if your child doesn't clear the jump. Alternatively, you could use elastic which is easily stretched. This will then give way easily.

You can attach the elastic between two chairs, a few inches off the ground. Place a mat on one side for the child to jump onto (this gives him a reason for jumping over).

At first take his hands until he gets the idea. You can gradually increase the height of the elastic or else move the mat further away, so that he has a 'long' jump as well as a 'high' jump.

Skipping – This follows on after the above activity. Here the child has to jump over the string while it's moving. First have two people slowly move the string along the ground. This gives the child plenty of time to see it coming and jump. Once he is able to jump over the string, raise it off the ground a little so that he has to jump higher, then move it a little quicker.

Later instead of just moving the string along the ground, you can bring it over his head. In this way, you will be gradually introducing him to the idea of skipping.

However, you should also encourage him to skip by himself as this gives him excellent practice at co-ordinating all his limbs (yes, boys as well as girls). This is a difficult skill for them to master and there are no short-cuts, yet often children persevere and success brings a great sense of achievement.

Tricycle

Riding a tricycle also gives the child practice at co-ordinating his leg movements (pedalling) and arm movements (steering) as well as helping his balance.

At first you will have to do much of the work for him. To save your back, tie a piece of rope to the handlebars and use this to pull him along. Encourage him to keep his feet on the pedals, for even if he isn't pedalling, he will experience the movement.

You could put a strip of elastic around his feet and the pedals. Or you might be able to make a back support to each pedal to stop his feet from slipping off. For example, remove the uppers from an old pair of sandals and attach the soles to the pedals (long carpet tacks can be used in rubber pedals). Now the child's heel can rest against the back of the sandal while the sole of his foot is over the pedal.

In time, the child will start to press on the pedals. Encourage him to do this by having him raise himself off the seat and 'stand on' the pedals.

Roller Skates

This is a much harder activity. Indeed many adults can't roller skate. But this is a very good activity to further develop the child's balance and co-ordination. As in all the previous activities, at first you will have to provide the child with lots of help. In many ways it's like learning to walk again and you could use some of the suggestions given in Booklet 2 (see p. 74) when helping your child learn to roller skate.

But try not to let him get too many bumps or you will put him off roller skates for life!

Now for some activities which involve lots of different actions:

Do This – All the child has to do is copy your actions; feet astride; hands in air, kneeling on ground etc. However, this activity is particularly good for getting him to do more difficult actions, such as standing on one leg.

Follow my Leader – The same as *Do This*, only this time all the actions are done on the move – walking, crawling, jumping up and down, hopping on one foot etc.

Try to link this activity with music. As the rhythm changes, you and the child vary your movements, e.g. when it's fast music, you run; when it's very slow, you take large steps; if it's quiet, you walk on tip-toe etc. You can weave a story around the actions, thereby making the activity imaginative play as well. This is described more fully in the section on *Imaginative Play* (see p. 192).

Obstacle Race – Lay out an 'obstacle course' around the house or garden; with a plank for walking on, an old chair to climb up and jump off, a 'tunnel' (old sack) to crawl under, string to jump over, suspended toys to jump up and catch and a bucket to throw them into etc. There are lots of things you can include. It may take him some time to get the idea of moving quickly from one thing to another, but if he sees you or other children do it, he will quickly learn.

Kicking the Ball

In Booklet 2 (see p. 80) we described some early kicking games with the child sitting, but it is important to extend these and also get him to kick when standing up. At first this will be difficult, for he will need a good sense of balance to kick the ball and still keep standing! Here are two ideas for helping him:

1. To give him the idea of kicking while standing, let him lean against furniture or a wall, or even just hold his hand. As he becomes more skilled at kicking, gradually move him away from the furniture so that he does it alone.
2. You can also make him kick by accident. For example, when he is walking along, roll the ball into his path and he can't help but knock it away; cheer when he does so.

If your child is able to kick a ball without falling over, here are some more advanced activities:

Directed Kicking – Having to kick a ball in a certain direction increases the child's control over his feet and legs. You can easily encourage this. At first, this can simply be through hitting the ball against a certain wall or part of the wall. Gradually, reduce the size of this (mark it out with chalk). Each time he hits it, he scores a goal and ten goals earn a drink of orange (or his favourite drink).

Alternatively, you can have him kicking the ball at objects which will fall over when hit, e.g. skittles, a piece of wood (2 feet square) held up by a rod (see Fig. 13).

Kick and Run – Once children can *easily* kick when standing, the next step is to have them kick when running. This

Wooden target held up by a stick to fall over when hit

Fig. 13

is much more difficult as it requires a lot of co-ordination and control of your legs. Often children will only run up to the ball, and stop dead before kicking the ball. It is not kicking on the run. Here's an idea for encouraging this. Attach a long piece of string to the ball with strong sticking tape. Now you can keep the ball moving by pulling on the string so that your child will have to keep moving if he is to kick it.

Throwing
You can tackle this in much the same way as kicking. At first children don't really throw anything; they just let objects roll out of their hands. One way of encouraging them to throw properly is to use a box for 'catching' the objects. At first you may have to cheat a bit and move the box as they throw to be sure the ball goes in, but having a 'target' can be an incentive to throw properly. As they progress, you can move the box further away.

Similarly, throwing a ball to knock over skittles etc., will help your child to learn to throw in a particular direction.

Remember you can use all sorts of things for throwing

(bean bags, balls of wool, crumpled paper) and as containers for catching (boxes, buckets, basins).

Alongside this, you can, of course, have him throwing things to you, especially if you also want him to learn to catch objects.

Catch It

This is a difficult skill for children to learn and indeed many adults are not very good at it. Of course, some objects are easier to catch than others; avoid small, round or slippery objects. (Bean bags are easier to catch than balls.) Indeed, if the child finds it difficult to hold or manipulate an object, then he will find greater difficulty in catching it. Here's a simple test you can try: Get your child to put his arms out in front of him; both together and palms upwards. Place the object on the middle of his fore-arm and see if he manages to grasp it with his hands. If he has difficulty doing so (it falls, or slips), then he will find it hard to catch it. Try with other objects and if it's always the same, it may be rather soon to have him catching.

The earliest practice at catching will come in activities like *Dangling a Carrot* (see p. 85) or when he is trying to grasp a dangling toy (see p. 113). For example, hold one of his dangling toys just out of reach. When your child reaches up to get it, let it drop into his hands. Once he has learnt to catch the toy, you can gradually increase the distance the toy falls before he can catch it.

Of course it is rather more difficult to catch an object when it is thrown to you. For one thing, it is much harder for children to judge the distance. So at first, don't throw from too far away.

To let him experience the idea of catching, you can start by almost doing it for him. That is, stand behind him and hold his arms out and slightly upward. Then have someone throw the ball into his arms. When he has caught it, cheer and make a fuss. You can then start getting him to do more himself, i.e. let him grasp the object to himself; then hold arms by himself waiting to catch etc.

Also if he is throwing the ball to you, stand with your arms out, ready to catch as he does (best to be on your knees or haunches to be sure of getting it).

As he becomes more proficient at this you can start having him put his arms further apart so that the object can fall between them. This will get him to catch properly. (NOTE: If the child has the use of only one arm, you can follow the same idea except that you have him put out his arm but bent at the elbow so that the objects can fall between his arm and chest.)

Team Games

Skills like kicking, throwing or catching are the basic elements of many team games such as football, rounders, cricket etc. Later in the book we will be describing how you can encourage your child to take part in team games (see p. 164).

SECTION 3: SKILFUL PLAY

INTRODUCTION TO SKILFUL PLAY

By skilful play we mean all those games and activities which require the skilful and controlled use of hand and eye.

Building a tower of bricks, playing tiddley-winks, fitting together pieces of jig-saw puzzle, playing ping-pong or constructing a model are all activities which demand considerable skill. This can only be gained by plenty of practice.

As adults we developed these skills so long ago that we may be inclined to take them for granted or become impatient with a clumsy child who breaks everything he touches. Yet watching a child unable to get a sweet out of a screw-top jar can help us to realise how frustrating it can be not to have these skills.

Skilful play begins long before a child can paint a picture or build a sand castle. A baby rhythmically banging his rattle in his pram is learning the skilful use of his limbs. Learning new skills continues all through life. Adults who enjoy embroidery or woodwork are engaged in a skilful form of recreation.

The Importance of Skilful Play

Here are five reasons for encouraging a child's skilful play:

1. *Skilful play enables a child to amuse himself constructively* – A child who cannot do much with his hands is very dependent upon an adult to amuse him. Instead of his toys getting broken or tangled up he needs to learn to make them do what he wants.

It is important to teach him the basic skills so that he can 'do-it-himself' rather than having to rely on you at every turn.

2. *Skilful play can reduce frustration* – A child can become very frustrated on seeing other people doing things which he cannot do such as cutting material, drawing a picture etc. The only way to reduce this frustration is to help him to develop these skills also.

3. *Skilful play leads to usefulness and independence in later life* – Not every handicapped person can become wholly independent but the more skilful he can be in the use of his hands the more useful and independent he becomes. Even ordinary everyday activities like wrapping up a parcel, unlocking a door, opening a tin or threading a needle require skill. You can help your child to develop these skills through the right kind of play. Without them he is wholly dependent and helpless.

4. *Developing new skills increases self-respect* – Great satisfaction and self-respect is gained from being able to do something well at every stage of development. Whether it is turning over the pages of a book or using a typewriter, we feel proud when we are able to do things properly.

Self-respect is a human right which can lead to respect from others.

5. *It is by handling materials that we learn* – The best way to learn is by doing. This is especially true in childhood. By handling materials skilfully a child learns about weight, shape, size, length, number, colour and sound.

Skilful play and the handicapped child
A very young baby or a handicapped child has much to learn before we can expect him to play even the simplest game demanding the skilful use of his hands.

A baby at birth appears almost entirely helpless and lacking in skills. He can root around to find the source of milk and make his discomfort known, but very little else. His arms and legs are uncontrolled. He flays them about when he gets excited but that is about all.

It is not like this with a young colt who can get up and run about a few hours after being born and recognises his mother and runs back to her. It takes the human infant a long time to get his limbs to obey him and his eyes to focus on distant objects.

At first, although he can pick things up and handle them, he will still be clumsy and ham fisted. Small toys will drop out of his hand, he may knock things over and have difficulty in getting them into the right position for opening a box and so on. The next step will be getting control of his fingers and thumbs so that he can pick up tiny objects. Most of the fine work which we need to do is done by holding tools with the sensitive tips of our fingers and thumbs. Think of threading a needle, or threading beads or writing.

It is easy for us to forget how complex these early efforts are. We do not usually have to teach them, the child seems to acquire them naturally. However, a handicapped child may take much longer before he can control his movements and may need help on the way. Depending on the degree of handicap he may just be slow or inclined to be clumsy or, if he is brain injured, have uncontrolled or restricted movement for years.

First, we need to know what he can and cannot do. Then we should devise many games to give him more practice in what he *can* do before introducing challenges to help him on to the next stage. For one stage will always depend on the stage before. He must be able to reach out and touch an object, for instance, before he can grasp it. He needs to be able to use both hands separately before he can hope to pass objects from hand to hand or use both hands together. Not only must he be able to control his hands, he must also use his eyes so that he can judge how far away an object is or how big it is. Until he can do this, you may find him, literally, reaching for the moon!

Encouraging Skilful Play
The rest of this section gives you details of activities you can use to encourage your child's skilful play. But as we noted earlier, the nature of skilful play changes as the child develops.

It is important therefore to pick activities which are suited to your child's level of development. If you pick activities which are too hard or too easy, your child will get no pleasure or benefit out of them. So, before starting on any games, you need to find out your child's present level in skilful play. To help you do this, we have prepared development charts.

Development Charts
You should find the charts useful in three ways:
1.   *The charts show the stages children go through in skilful play* – The items have been arranged in the order children usually develop them; the earliest activity is given first and the most advanced last. Thus as you read down the page, you will see the stages in the development of children's skilful play.
2.   *The charts give you a framework for observing your child* – The charts highlight specific skills which you can look for in your child, or activities which you should try with him to see whether he can or cannot do them. By doing this you will learn more about your child's present level of development.
3.   *The charts provide a means of recording your child's progress* – Beside each item you can record whether your child can (tick YES) or cannot (tick NO) do that item. If you go through the charts at regular intervals, say every six months (marking the items with different coloured pens on each occasion), you will be able to record his progress in skilful play. This will be a great source of encouragement to you.

We suggest that you now read through the charts. Then over the next few days observe your child and record whether he can or cannot do the items as listed. Once you have done this, we can then guide you to suitable games and activities for your child.

Choosing Skilful Play Activities
We have grouped the skilful play activities into two booklets:
Booklet 1: *Taking Hold*
Booklet 2: *Clever Hands*

Skilful Play Charts

Watches and follows a dangling toy moved in front of face	YES	NO	
Grasps toys, e.g. simple play with rattle	YES	NO	
Reaches out and picks up small toys straight away	YES	NO	*Booklet 1*
Passes a toy from one hand to the other	YES	NO	*Taking Hold* *p. 105*
Bangs with stick (or spoon, hammer etc.) on another 'toy' (tin, box, ball etc.)	YES	NO	
Picks up small objects (e.g. small pieces of string) between finger and tip of thumb	YES	NO	

Builds a tower of three bricks	YES	NO	
Scribbles in circles and straight lines	YES	NO	
Removes screw-top from bottle	YES	NO	*Booklet 2* *Clever Hands*
Threads six beads onto a lace	YES	NO	*p. 120*
Tries to cut with scissors	YES	NO	
Draws a 'man' on request, showing legs and head	YES	NO	

You will have noticed the titles of the booklets alongside the items in the charts. Look back at the charts: if you have ticked NO to any of the items covered by the first booklet, then we suggest you go first to Booklet 1 (p. 105) and try some of the activities given there. You should also read Booklets 1 and 2 in *Exploratory Play* (p. 30).

If the first item you ticked NO is covered by Booklet 2 or if you ticked all the items YES, then look at Booklet 2 first (p. 120). Leave out Booklet 1.

Once you start the games, note carefully your child's reaction. If he makes no attempt to join in or becomes frustrated or distressed, then you are probably expecting too much of him. Try some 'simpler' activities. On the other hand, if he joins in readily but soon stops, it could be that the game is too easy and he's bored. Try some more 'advanced' activities. Avoid becoming too ambitious and turning what should be fun and recreation into drudgery! Never discourage your child from playing very simple games if he enjoys them. These help to give him greater mastery over his environment. If you are introducing something more difficult and novel, remember not to go on too long the first time. Always try to stop the game before he tires of it, and then it will remain something special to look forward to.

BOOKLET 1: TAKING HOLD

Before a child can take part in many of the skilful activities such as drawing, building bricks, etc. he needs to have certain skills. In particular he needs to be able to:
1. Look at objects and follow them if they move.
2. Reach out for objects.
3. Hold objects in his hand.
4. Use finger *and thumb* to grasp objects.

  This booklet is concerned with games and activities to help your child acquire these early skills. As there are a lot of things to cover, this booklet will be longer than most. However, we have divided it into four parts, each one dealing with a different skill.

Part 1: *Look for it* (p. 106) – describes activities to encourage children to look and follow objects.

Part 2: *Reach out* (p. 109) – describes activities to encourage , reaching.

Part 3: *Getting a grip* (p. 112) – describes activities to encourage grasping.

Part 4: *All fingers and thumbs* (p. 116) – describes activities to encourage use of fingers and thumbs.

General Hints
But before you start, here are some general points to bear in mind:
1. *Nothing to do or see* – So long as your child is *awake* he should have something to do or see. Make sure that when he makes a movement *something happens*. This will encourage him to try again.

2. *A change of scene* – Make sure your child does not lie for hours on his back staring at the ceiling. It is enough to send anyone to sleep! Keep giving him a change of scene; change his position, let him watch you at work and so on. Take him on a guided tour to feel the curtains, handle dough etc.

3. *Bring it to him* – A baby or child with weak muscles cannot help himself. You must bring a variety of objects to him. Put them in his hands and let him feel them against his cheek.

4. *Passive movement* – Your child may move very little. To start with you may have to move his arms and legs for him. Clap his hands, bicycle his legs but encourage him to finish the movement on his own. If your child is physically handicapped, seek advice from your doctor or physiotherapist.

5. *Support for the handicapped* – A handicapped child is sometimes unable to sit up or support his head or change his position. In his case it is important to arrange supports so that he can sit up and handle new toys. Often suitable rests and supports can be made of expanded polystyrene cut to size and fastened together with special adhesive, e.g. Evostik 83 (the ordinary variety is not suitable). Then cover with cloth or plastic. Alternatively you could use a 'sag-bag' (see p. 32). Try to get the advice of a physiotherapist or doctor as to the best kind of support.

Part 1: Look for it

Following moving objects – Even before a child can move around, he learns to follow moving objects with his eyes and to turn his head in the direction of sounds. A handicapped child has to be encouraged to follow sounds and objects. Here are some suggestions for doing this:

Head turning to sounds – Novelty is important here. Rustle some paper, or ring a bell or squeak a little toy, first on the right hand side of his head and then on the left and see whether he will turn to the sound. Keep the objects out of sight. (If your child never seems to turn towards a sound unless he can see where it comes from, you should have his hearing tested.)

Other ways of helping him to track the sounds are to use 'musical' toys: tins and containers full of peas or beans which make an interesting sound when rattled; tapping on a tin with a spoon; rattling a bunch of keys or pouring water from one cup to another. Galt's sell 'tins' which make animal noises when turned over and these are very useful for getting the child 'searching' for sounds. Also, most toy shops sell small musical boxes which play when a string is pulled.

Variety is the great thing. This will arouse his interest and he will begin to know what it is which makes the different sounds.

Be sure that you do not always rattle things on the same side but encourage him to turn to the left and to the right, to look up in search for the sound and to look down.

Tracking – When you are watching a distant car you can easily lose track of it if you stop concentrating. A young child cannot track even a slow moving object in front of his face – this is a skill he has to learn.

In the first place, you have to start by engaging his interest. Dangle a little toy, or a balloon, or a shiny tin or little mirror in front of him. Once he is interested, start moving the object slowly, sometimes to the right and sometimes to the left so that he must move his eyes and then his head in order to follow it. Let the toy disappear and reappear behind a chair or curtain sometimes. When your child is tracking objects which are near to him, try moving them a little further away.

If it is difficult to capture his interest, buy or try making a paper windmill which will turn around when you blow on it and, once he is watching it, start moving it from side to side (see Fig. 14).

Other suggestions – One of the first things babies will follow with their eyes is a moving light. See whether he will follow the light of a moving torch.

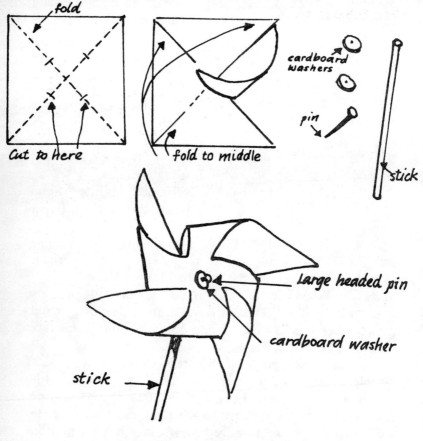

Making a paper windmill

Fig. 14

Try propping him up in front of a mirror and let him watch his own movements.

Tie a tin or torch onto a string and start it swinging in front of his eyes. You can also buy toys on springs which move up and down and these will encourage eye movement.

Part 2: Reach out

Toys to encourage movement and reaching – At first, a baby may not seem to be interested in the world around him. He cannot reach out and touch anything even if he wants to. His arms and legs move but they seem to have a 'mind of their own'. However, we can help him to start to move his arms and legs more purposefully by making it worthwhile, i.e. something happens when he does. Note the movements your child usually makes. Now put rattles or other baubles in the path of these movements. Hitting these will encourage him to repeat the movement. Or you can place an easily squeakable toy where his hand or foot is likely to drop. This will start to capture his interest and he will repeat his involuntary action and get it under control. Even a piece of rustling paper can be placed on the cot, where he is likely to kick it.

Moving Ornament – Particularly useful for encouraging your child to move his arms (and legs) is the ornament shown in Fig. 15. You can buy these in 'fancy goods' shops. This

Moving ornament

Fig. 15

consists of small coloured balls on fine wire. If your child touches it with his hand or arm, it will set the balls crashing into each other. He not only sees the effect of his movement, but hears it as well!

Kelly dolls – Kelly dolls are large plastic toys which make a musical sound when they are pushed. They are weighted so that when struck they rock backwards and forwards but do not fall over.

Children find these fascinating and they are encouraged to use first one hand and then the other to get them rocking and to hear the music.

Squeaky toys – You will have to search around until you find very soft rubber toys which squeak easily. Tie a piece of tape around the toy and stitch onto the coverlet wherever your child's hand usually falls when he is flaying around. Do not leave the toy always on the same side – change it round.

Rustling toys – Try screwing up different kinds of paper, grease proof paper, brown paper etc. Stitch these to the cover of the cot or pram. If loosely screwed up, they will still make a sound even after they are touched.

Patchwork quilts – You might like to make a little patch-work quilt to put over your child's cot or pram. Use fairly large pieces of material (about 3 inch squares) and make some of furry material, others of plastic or fablon and one of wool and use a variety of colours. These patches will feel different to the touch and this will encourage him to reach out and explore with his hands.

Musical mitts – Sew a little bell *firmly* onto the tip of each of your baby's mitts or child's gloves. Use one mitt or glove at a time to begin with. Tie the mitt or glove onto one hand and leave the other free. Each time your child moves his hands this will make a sound which should arrest his attention. Soon he will be moving his hand *in order* to make the interesting sound, he will start to look for the source of the sound, to move his hand gently or perhaps to shake it energetically. He may explore with his other hand until he touches the bell and this is an important step forward. It is vital to encourage a child to use both hands. On another day put the mitt on his other hand and leave the first hand free. On a cold day when he is outside, put both mitts on at once. Start him going by taking his hand and shaking it.

Dangling toys – Dangling toys, because they are always moving and changing shape and colour, are ideal for encouraging your child to reach out and eventually to grasp and handle objects.

If there is a handyman in the house (or handywoman) get him to make a light wooden frame which can be bolted onto a cot, chair or pram. The sides of the frame should be out of the child's reach (see Fig. 1). The toys can then be suspended from this. You can use cord, although strong, round elastic is better as this makes the toys bob up and down. Adjust the length of the elastic, so that your child can reach out and touch the toys. If he swipes at them, this will get them bobbing up and down. You can dangle all sorts of things. For example:

(a) cream cartons (filled with peas)
(b) crumpled paper
(c) balls of wool
(d) little bells
(e) squeaky toys.

If you introduce only one or two at a time, you will be able to watch and see which 'toy' your child prefers. Do not always put this favourite toy in the same position. This will only encourage your child to use one hand or always to turn to the same side. What you want to encourage is overall development with the use of both hands separately and together. So vary the position of the toys on the frame. Some children are most active when there are only a few dangling toys, others when there are many. See which your child prefers.

If your child gets bored with one lot of toys, take these away and dangle another set.

Part 3: Getting a grip

(NOTE: If your child has great difficulty in moving either of his hands, use these games in consultation with a physio-therapist.)

Even before your child is reaching out and picking up objects you can help his grasping. Encourage him to open and close his hand; open it for him and tickle his palm. Close his hand over a smooth length of dowelling and gently turn it round. When he starts to grasp this on his own, start pulling it away very gently to strengthen his grasp. Do this with other toys or pieces of cloth etc.

Pull yourself up – Encourage your child to grasp your out-stretched fingers with his two hands and gradually try lifting him into a sitting position. Or you can encourage him to hold onto a stick of dowelling with both hands and similarly lift him into a sitting position.

Row the boat – Sit on the floor with your child between your legs. Take hold of his hands and both gently rock back-wards and forwards; just as if you were rowing a boat. When he is used to this, you can then get him to grasp your fingers. He will then have to hold on to keep the boat 'moving'! This will help to strengthen his grasp. While you are playing this game, you can sing a song – a sea shanty perhaps?

Dangling toys – The dangling toys we described earlier are ideal for encouraging the child to grasp (see p. 111). You can use different toys to let him practise different sorts of grasping actions, e.g. long thin toys require a different grasp from large round ones.

Two hands together – For most skilful occupations we have to use both hands, even if one is only holding down a piece of paper and the other is writing; or one is holding a cup and the other is drying it. This ability to use both hands together is the foundation of future skills.

Clap hands – By clapping your baby's hands together and crossing them over from side to side you will be helping him to locate and use his hands together. Later play hand over hand (you put one hand flat on the table, he places his over yours and then you put your other hand over his and he puts his second hand over yours – when the pile is complete, you slip your first hand out from the bottom of the pile and place it on the top and then he does the same). Then you can start playing pat-a-cake with him. All these games should increase his skill at using his two hands together.

Bobbing sausages – Sausage shapes are particularly easy for children to handle. You can easily make some 'sausages' out of gaily coloured pieces of cloth stuffed with old tights, rice or foam. They should be about three to four inches in length.

Add little bells onto the top of the sausages for good measure and suspend them in front of the child. Start them bobbing up and down – one near his left hand and one near his right. If he does not try to grasp the sausages put one in his hand and then try putting the other in his other hand. At first, he will always drop the first one. If he is only using one hand (say his right), move the sausages and encourage him to use the other hand as well. You may even have to restrain one hand in order that he may use the other.

You can leave him to practise on his own once he has begun to try to grasp these sausages. The elastic makes them bob up and down and should hold his interest. Soon he will learn to hold them in both hands at the same time and even to pass them from hand to hand. This is a great step forward.

You can use other sorts of dangling toys but try to have two of the same, otherwise the child may prefer one of the two and not want to grasp both.

Using both hands – Sometimes handicapped children are reluctant to use one of their hands. You should *not* encourage this.

When your child is on the floor or lying in a bed or couch, make sure you leave interesting toys and objects on either side of him as this encourages him to make use of either hand to reach and *grasp* them. You may even need to place the toys so that he *has* to use the reluctant hand to get them. Hand toys to him from the side he does not usually use.

Large toys – You can also get a child to use his 'reluctant' hand by giving him toys which are too large to hold in one hand. For example, tie a large baby ball onto a string. Dangle this in front of your child. He will need both hands to hold it. When he is able to grasp it you could try swinging it gently so that he has to catch it as it comes towards him. Later you could increase the swing.

Pram toys – Many baby shops sell interesting strings of pram toys for a child to touch or handle. Handicapped children may need this kind of play when they are older and bigger. You can use an expanding curtain rod or a piece of dowelling and stretch this across a wheel chair or ordinary chair or sofa, wherever your child is propped up (see Fig. 16).

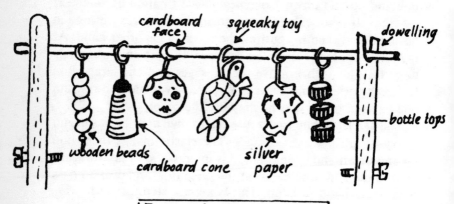

Frame for pram or cot

Fig. 16

You can thread all kinds of toys and objects onto this frame; baby rattles, teething rings, large beads, little plastic cups and cotton reels. You could also tie a loop onto a baby bell and thread this on so that it rings when you move it along.

Change the toys quite often. Children like novelty, and different toys help different grasping movements.

Come back – Often children do not get much practise grasping, simply because when they drop toys, they cannot reach them. They have to wait until you hand the toys back to them or put the toys within their reach. If the toys did not roll away, the child would get more practise at grasping. Here are some ideas you could use for doing this:

Sucker Toys – A toy with a sucker base can be bought at most baby shops. You can leave your child to play with this but make sure he is not able to dislodge it. It will encourage him to use both hands; as he bangs it with his right hand, it will lean towards the left and encourage him to bang it back.

Tethered Toys – Fasten small lengths of string or elastic to some of your child's toys. Attach the ends to hooks or screws on a piece of wood which you can firmly attach to a table or to the floor. This will keep the toys within your child's reach, even if he throws them!

Tray – A tray or bed table with a specially raised edge is useful. You can seat your child at this and know that the toys will not roll off; at least not accidentally.

Revolving pictures – A revolving picture box will keep a child active for quite a long time and also give him a change of scene to look at. You can easily make this toy using a square cardboard box, a length of dowelling and a wooden base (see Fig. 17).

This box can be fastened down on a tray or table with Blu-tack or doublesided carpet tape. It should be put in a convenient position for the child to flip around at a touch. Pictures should be pasted onto the sides of the box and often changed. A small bell could be fixed inside the box to ring as it revolves.

Toy dropping – Most children love to play a dropping game – they often wear you out by dropping toys out of a pram or cot and waiting for you to pick them up. You can play similar games and help them in their skilful use of both hands. Find a large tin, bowl or box and a collection of small toys or household objects which make an interesting sound when dropped into the container. Place the container so that your child can easily drop toys into it, but place it sometimes at

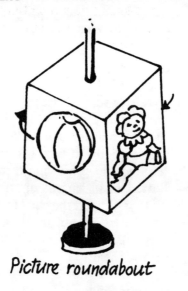

Picture roundabout

Fig. 17

his right hand side and sometimes at his left. Hand toys to him at the side further away from the container, this will encourage him to pass toys from hand to hand or to cross his arm to the opposite side of his body, in order to drop the toy into the box. Vary the sizes of toys and containers.

Part 4: All fingers and thumbs

Most toys we provide for babies or for handicapped older children are big and strong and can be easily grasped with the whole hand. We seldom provide them with tiny objects to handle. This is only natural for we are fearful that they may put these objects in their mouths and swallow them.

Yet a child has to learn to pick up small objects between his finger and thumb and he will not learn to do this without practice. So he must have tiny objects to experiment with. If you are afraid he will put these in his mouth, then make sure that the objects are edible and then it will not matter.

Also, he is more likely to persevere in trying to pick them up if the reward is pleasant.

Small sweets can be used but if you do not wish to ruin your child's teeth why not try small nuts, short lengths of spaghetti, pieces of biscuit, raisins, potato sticks, peas, and so on. Arrange them so that he has to pick them up one by one. If he tries to scoop a handful, only give him one at a time. He is not likely to spoil his appetite for meals in this way.

Try giving him a tray full of little lengths of coloured wool to pick up. Find some little bottles and boxes and see if he can take small objects out of them.

Finger Games – Lots of finger games will help your child in the skilful use of his fingers and thumbs. Touch your thumb with each finger at a time and see if he will copy this. Draw a little face on each of his nails and get him to make a fist and then stand his fingers up one at a time.

If you have a piano, let him try to strike the keys gently using each finger in turn, or later let him do this on a type-writer. If you draw a different face on each of his nails, you can say 'It's daddy's turn to play ... It's mummy's turn' and so on. This will encourage him to use one finger at a time, rather than banging with his whole hand.

Turn of the Screw – When a child is able to pick objects up between finger and thumb and also is starting to use both hands together, games should be played which involve screwing and unscrewing.

At first, the child should not be expected both to hold the object and unscrew the toy etc. A collection of objects for screwing and unscrewing can be assembled and stuck onto a board.

Unscrewing – Mount some bolts onto a board and screw nuts onto them. Show him how to unscrew the nuts. At first make this very easy with the nut very near to the top of the bolt so that it will come off easily. Gradually make it more difficult. (Galt's sell a selection of screwing toys.)

Containers with Lids – Collect a number of clean containers with lids (screw top jars, cocoa tins, boxes etc. yoghurt cartons etc.). Give your child one at a time with a little sweet or nut at the bottom. See whether he can get this out.

You will have to grade these containers in order of difficulty. The first of the series should be a jar or clear container without a lid so that he sees the sweet and only has to turn the jar upside down in order to obtain it.

When he can do this, give him a tin or carton without a lid and see whether he tips this up straight away. Next, give him a clear jar with a plastic screw top, unscrew this part of the way and see whether he can do the rest. If he cannot, hold his hand and unscrew the top with him. Then give him one to do himself.

Go on in the same way with this, show him how to prise off the top with a coin and then leave him to it.

The danger here is to give the child too much help. Leave him with the container for some time before you intervene unless he is getting too violently frustrated. Let him work

Picture wheel

Fig. 18

things out for himself and do not stop him every time he tries the 'wrong' way.

Later you could give him harder puzzles, for example, boxes with catches etc. (see *Treasure Chest*, p. 228).

Picture Wheel – Cut out a circle of stiff card. Pierce a hole through the middle and stick a cocktail stick through the hole.

Divide the circle into four and paint a picture in each quarter. Mount this wheel in a box so that it can be turned like a top. Cut a little window in the box so that just one picture appears at a time (see Fig. 18).

Turning the stick to find a new picture helps your child to use his fingers skilfully.

Jack in the Box – Find a little metal pill box with a screw top. Get a handyman to solder a small spring into the base of the tin and fasten a little toy onto the top. Screw the top on. Show your child how to unscrew the top and let the toy jump out like a 'jack-in-the-box'. Or you could use Kiddicraft's toy, 'Billie and his Barrels'. This consists of different sized barrels which screw apart so that they can fit inside one another.

BOOKLET 2: CLEVER HANDS

The activities in this booklet are mainly for children who can look for, reach out, and grasp even quite small toys. If you feel your child needs more practice at doing any of these, then see the activities in Booklet 1 (p. 105).

We have divided this booklet into four parts. Each part deals with a particular type of skilful play activity.

Part 1: Using tools (p. 120) – describes activities which require the child to use a 'tool'.

Part 2: In it goes (p. 124) – describes stacking and threading games.

Part 3: Build it up (p. 128) – describes games and activities which involve building or constructing things.

Part 4: Drawing (p. 130) – describes games and activities centred around drawing but including cutting and pasting.

In each part, we describe very early activities and show how they become increasingly complex. So within *each part*, you should find some activities which are suited to your child's present level of development.

Part 1: Using tools

Man differs from other animals in that he can use tools as an extension of his hands. If he cannot reach an object, he can get it with a rake. He does not have to dig in the earth like a mole but can use a fork.

It is important to help your child to use tools skilfully. You are probably already teaching him to use a spoon or spoon and fork at meal times and know how difficult this is for some children.

Why not introduce games with tools? Here are some suggestions which he should enjoy.

Hammering Games – Get some upturned tins or boxes or a bucket and a little stick, dowel rod, pencil, or little rubber hammer. Place the tins etc. around the child and place the small stick in his hand. Hold his hand or arm and show him how to tap the tins around him, first to the left and then to the right. Later you could hang a tin on a string above him and tap this too. Gradually reduce your help until he is vigorously banging the tins in all directions. This should be quite a strenuous game; keep changing the positions of the tins and keep it moving. Do not leave the stick always in the same hand. A good idea is to play this game to music and start banging to a simple rhythm.

Drumsticks – This time two hammers or sticks are required. Persuade your child to hold one in each hand. Some children are reluctant to use both hands and you may have to help him by steering one to bang while he uses the other or you may even have to steer both hands at first.

As before, you need plenty of objects around in different positions: drums, xylophone, tins, cymbals, bells which make interesting sounds when hit. As he gets more expert, you can encourage different rhythms with each hand.

Also hang some tins up so that he can bang these from different angles.

Other Hammering Games – When your child becomes more skilful at hitting with a hammer, get him one of the hammering games on the market. These will help to develop his skill further. There are a number of different types:

Hammer balls – here the child has to hammer balls through a hole. The ball later re-appears down a chute for the child to hammer it through again.

Hammer pegs – this is the well-known toy, where the child hammers the pegs, then turns the toy over so that he can hammer the pegs back again. Most toy shops sell this game.

Make-a-Picture – You can also buy a rather different sort of hammering game. This consists of different coloured shapes which the child nails onto a board with tacks in order to make a 'picture'. Most toy shops sell these or you can easily make your own.

Cut out some bright coloured shapes from cardboard or balsa wood. Buy a box of large headed carpet tacks and get a sheet of expanded polystyrene about two feet square and two inches thick. Give your child a light wooden hammer and let him attach the shapes to the polystyrene with the tacks.

Sorting Games with Tools – Introduce a simple sorting game. You do not need to buy anything for this, only to collect a box full of junk. For instance, collect bottle tops and corks or large buttons or wooden beads or walnuts etc. Provide two or more plastic boxes and a tray.

Place a few of these objects (say, bottle tops and buttons) in front of the child on the tray and get him to sort these into the appropriate boxes. You could put a sample in each box to start him off. When he has got the idea of the game and can sort objects confidently, then introduce some variations into the game.

Collect some tools, i.e. a pair of sugar tongs, plastic spoons and forks, a fish slice.

Instead of allowing your child to pick the objects up and sort them into the boxes, he must now pick them up with the tongs, say. Prevent him when he tries to use his fingers instead and hold his hand on the tongs.

Another time give him a spoon and make the game one of picking the objects up in this, then use a fish slice.

Sorting Games with Obstacles – Sorting games such as have already been described can be made more enjoyable and also increase skills by introducing obstacles into the game. These obstacles should be easy at first but gradually they should become more difficult. Once the game is started and the sorting is under way then the objects can be presented to the child in a bottle, he must get them out by turning the bottle upside down before he can sort the objects. Later he has the objects presented in a screw-top jar and must remove the lid before tipping the objects out and sorting them. As he becomes more proficient, he will discover how to prise off a tin lid with a coin (you may have to help him the first time) and even open boxes with a hasp. Make sure you do not intervene too soon, a child learns best when he discovers how to do things himself.

Hoopla – Hoopla games from toy shops are often too difficult for handicapped children when played in the conventional way, i.e. when the children have to throw the rings onto the hooks.

Here is another way of playing such a game. Provide the child with a rod (a length of dowelling will do). He has to get the ring onto the rod and then steer it so that it slips down the rod onto the hook (see Fig. 19).

Once your child is able to get the rings onto the hooks, see if he can take them off again. At first let him pick them off with his fingers but later see if he can get them off with the stick – this is harder than getting them on!

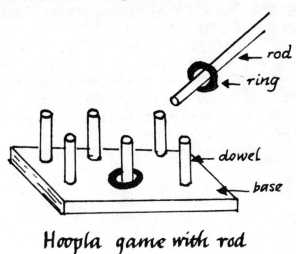

Hoopla game with rod

Fig. 19

Bat and Ball Games – These usually involve striking a moving ball with a bat, but this is quite difficult for a child to learn. However, even very young children delight in hitting a stationary ball.

At first use a large bat and ball, but ensure that they are quite light. Most shops now sell light plastic cricket bats, golf clubs or tennis rackets especially for little children.

You may need to start with an extra large ball, in foam or plastic. However, as your child gets better at hitting the ball with the bat you could introduce the smaller ball. Equally, you could introduce more challenging bats, perhaps starting with a tennis racket and then a cricket bat and then a golf club.

Opportunities for Using Tools – We have suggested some games for using tools, but don't forget the many natural opportunities for tool-use in and around the house, e.g. sweeping the floor, digging the garden, painting the fence, washing the car, rolling out dough, washing the pots, picking out sugar lumps with tongs and spooning out rice into a bowl. Give your child an opportunity to play with these tools or with toy replicas and to watch you at work and copy you before expecting him to use tools properly. Given this opportunity, he will be quicker to learn when the time comes. These opportunities will not only provide extra practice in skills he has already learned, but they will also allow him to develop new skills.

Part 2: On it goes

Putting rings onto a stick or threading beads onto a lace, often has a particular fascination for children. These are also ideal ways of developing your child's fine-motor skills, i.e. delicate use of fingers and thumbs.

Clown Stack – This is particularly useful for the hyperactive child or a child who throws objects around and does not play with them constructively. A wooden box is used for this with a dowel rod inserted on the top. A clown's face is painted on the box and holes made for the eyes. A battery is used so that torch bulbs light up in the eyes when a switch is pressed – if a bleeper is also used, this toy is doubly effective.

The child's hand should at first be guided to putting a ring over the rod. Each time the ring is put on the rod the clown is made to light up and bleep.

Later, the child should be encouraged to put the rings on by himself. When he does, the clown lights up! You can increase his concentration by deciding only to 'flash' and 'bleep' when three rings have gone on instead of only one. Later you could only 'flash' when all the rings have gone on.

When your child can stack the clown with a rod on his head, you can introduce him to a harder task. Now have a stacking rod sticking out on either side of the clown (see Fig. 20). You may find your child is puzzled by this at first and searches for the rod on the top of the clown's head.

dowel

Clown with side sticks

Fig. 20

Guide his hands so that he finds how to use both hands with the two sticks. At first 'flash' the clown for each ring and then for every three, every five etc.

Harder Stacking – When your child has mastered the simple ring-stacking, with or without the clown, you can think about harder stacking toys. You can buy many different types in toy shops, e.g. those which have rings of different sizes which make a pyramid.

Fisher-Price make a stacking-toy which rocks backwards and forwards. This requires more skill to put the rings on for the stack does not stand still.

Remember in playing with these toys children have to learn how to get the rings off as well as on to the stack. Give them time to explore for themselves.

You may also notice them trying to push the ring through the bottom of the stack; they know where it should end up but they cannot cope with the detour involved in getting it there. Once again, give them the freedom to make mistakes and to correct them by themselves.

You can make your own ring-stacking toys with wooden dowel or thin metal rods set in a wooden base. By using rods of various thickness you can grade the difficulty level of the toy from very easy to hard. Our book – *Let's Make Toys* – gives detailed instructions for making and using such ring-stacking toys.

Morgenstern Developmental Toys – E.S.A. market some more difficult stacking and threading toys (see Fig. 21) which

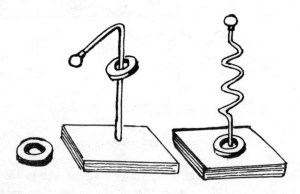

Some Morgenstern stacking toys

Fig. 21

are particularly useful for physically handicapped children as they have to keep adjusting their hand and wrist position in order to get the ring down the twisted rod. It may be difficult to motivate a child to persevere with some of these toys. A *bleeper* added to the toy will probably increase his willingness to persevere. It should only bleep when the ring is at the bottom of the stack.

Starting to Thread – Threading is very like stacking except that the rod and the rings have both to be held and guided correctly.

When your child is able to stack, start him on graded threading. For this you will need lengths of different thicknesses of dowel with thick cord attached (see Fig. 22). To start with, let him thread the rings from the stacking toy onto the cord (you may have to glue one ring onto the end of the rod

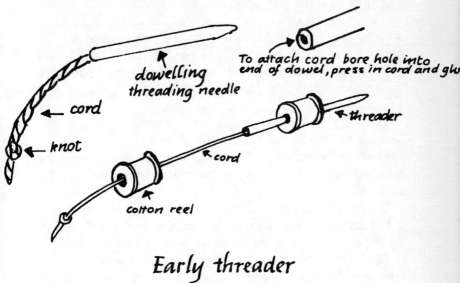

dowelling
threading needle

To attach cord bore hole into end of dowel, press in cord and glu

← *cord*

← *knot*

threader

cord

cotton reel

Early threader

Fig. 22

to prevent it falling off the end). Get your child both to thread and *unthread* the rings (unthreading is harder than threading). Then use thin dowelling and cotton reels for threading.

The next stage of threading will be large, wooden beads on shoe laces.

Part 3: Build it up

There are many constructional play sets in toy shops, e.g. Meccano, Lego. But before you can expect your child to play with these, he needs to practise with much simpler activities such as the following:

Towers of Bricks – Once your child is able to pick objects up and place them down again, you can start giving him some small, wooden bricks (1″) to play with. It is best to give him only a few at first. Give them to him in a box so that he will learn to take them out and *later* to put them back again. You can then turn the box upside down. Putting a brick on top of the upturned box is the beginning of stacking or building with bricks. You could then introduce a larger, wooden brick and let him place the small one on this. Until he has had practice doing this, he will not be ready to place a small brick on another small one. Do this in front of him and let him knock it off.

Then try with three bricks and gradually increase the number so that he can build a tower.

Once he has the idea of building, you can start varying the building materials – you can use cotton reels, boxes, milk cartons, tins etc.

Do not let the play become too mechanical. Make sure it is fun and try to introduce variations, e.g. building the tower on the bed instead of the floor, or even on Dad's tummy!

Babies' soft bricks can also be built into towers and, if a strong string is fastened on to the bottom brick of the tower, a pull on the string will still make the tower come tumbling down. Reluctant 'players' often find this hard to resist. Introduced gently, this game may help children to inhibit a 'startle' reflex when they find the bricks cannot hurt them.

Brick Trains – When your child has started building you

can show him how to position bricks in a line to make a train and push it along making train noises. Again, use different materials, larger bricks, boxes etc. and use your imagination.

Constructional Toys – There are many pull-along, wooden toys on the market with wooden 'men' or shapes that fit into holes in the 'car' and these toys help the child to judge sizes and also develop manual skills when putting the 'men' in place. Some of these toys take to pieces by means of large

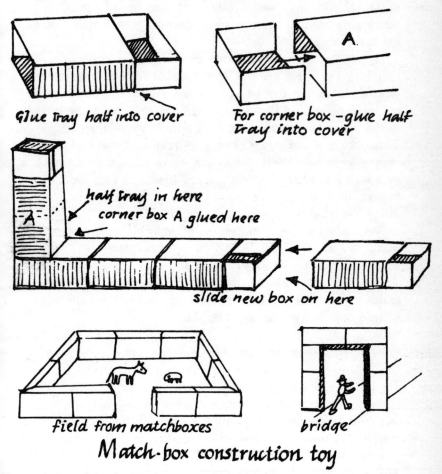

Glue tray half into cover

For corner box – glue half tray into cover

half tray in here
corner box A glued here

slide new box on here

field from matchboxes

bridge

Match-box construction toy

Fig. 23

nuts and bolts. Your child will find it easier to take them to pieces than to reassemble them. It is a skilled job getting the nut in the right place. Once building with simple bricks and boxes is well advanced, then locking plastic bricks (Alocubes made by E.S.A. for example) can be introduced. When a child is able to fit these together, you can consider buying him a set of Lego.

However, you do not have to rely on expensive toys. Many of the things that we throw away are equally good for developing manual skills and also encourage creativity. Here are some suggestions.

Match box toy – Everybody can acquire a collection of matchboxes. These are not very suitable for children unless treated. Here is a toy you can make. Cover the boxes with coloured paper and then ideally varnish them. Stick the trays to the boxes so that they are protruding by half their length. These boxes make inexpensive constructional material when clipped over one another and can make a train or a bridge or a wall etc. With a little ingenuity these can even be made to go round corners (see Fig. 23). For greater durability, try filling the trays with polystyrene or Polyfilla.

Wood blocks – Small offcuts are often available from wood-yards, or a length of wooden batten can be cut into short lengths and sanded down. If small hooks and eyes are screwed into the ends of these blocks, they can be hooked together into trains or cars and trailers. By hooking and unhooking these a child becomes increasingly skilful.

Part 4: Drawing

Scribbling, drawing and painting are not only skilful; they are also a means of self-expression.

Using a pencil, crayon or brush, and being able to cut out and paste pictures into a book are skills which make an excellent preparation for school.

A child needs to be able to scribble before he can write his own name or form figures.

Scribbling – As soon as your child can hold a crayon and has started to experiment with banging one thing on another etc. he should be encouraged to scribble. At first it is best to anchor a largish piece of paper down onto a flat table top with Blu-tack until he learns to hold it down himself. Do not expect him to spend much time scribbling at first but give him the experience for a few minutes a day. If he does not scribble then hold his hand and move it round so that the crayon makes a mark. Do not expect him to draw shapes or copy them or lines until he is scribbling freely on his own. He will be encouraged if you sit down and draw and colour beside him. When he is ready show him by holding and guiding his hand, how to make a circle. Do not overdo this but praise him if he makes an enclosed shape and discuss what this might be – a ball, a rock, a sausage etc. You can also show him how to colour with the side of the crayon. Squares and triangles are more difficult as the child has to start a line in one direction and then change direction abruptly at the corners.

You can help a child's ability to control the direction of his pencil or crayon by giving him practice in joining matching pictures.

Picture Joining – The simplest game consists of only two pictures, e.g. two cats. Show him that he has to draw a line from one cat to the other. If need be, hold his hand and if he starts scribbling, take the paper away. Later you can prepare a piece of paper as in Fig. 24. He has to join the same pictures together. Give him plenty of practice. You do not need elaborate pictures, in fact, it is best to draw them in front of him rather than have them ready prepared. At first let him join only a few objects but later you could add many more. Not only does this help his hand-eye co-ordination, it also helps him to identify and match pictures and talk about them.

As soon as you introduce your child to crayoning or drawing, establish a routine of putting each crayon back in its own

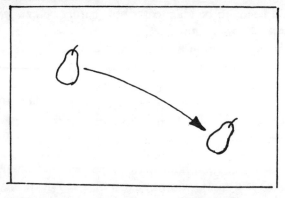

Simple picture joining

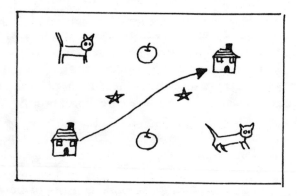

More difficult picture joining

Fig. 24

place before using the next, or putting the tops on colouring sticks before putting them away. Many children do not look after their tools, but they can get into the habit of doing so if this habit is inculcated right at the beginning.

Painting – Start with only one of the primary colours (red, blue or yellow). Mix poster or powder colour with water in a screw-top jar (e.g. a squat jar like a honey pot is best), or better still, use non-spill paint pots (obtainable from Galt's).

Use a soft but not too fine a brush and large sheets of white or brown paper (18″ × 24″ is a good size).

Attach a sheet of paper to a board and put this on an easel if you have one, or against the back of a washable kitchen chair. Give your child some clean water and a damp cloth to wipe his hands. At first, do not try to paint anything but guide your child in the technique of putting paint on paper gently and evenly without it dripping down. You can pretend you are painting the wall! When you have shown him the techniques let him practice with one colour for some time before introducing another colour. When you introduce the second colour also introduce another brush so that the colours do not get mixed up unintentionally. Show him how to get rid of surplus water on the side of the jar before painting. Your child will need a painting smock or one of his father's shirts when he is painting – remember to put down newspapers or a large polythene sheet on the floor if it is something which will spoil.

It is best to make painting rather a special treat and also not to let it go on too long each day. If you pack up after a short time your child will look forward to another try next day and is less likely to fool about with the paint or water. If he shows any tendency to do this, do not scold him but pack the painting things up and put them away until next time. When your child has got to the point that he can manage three colours without making too much of a mess, show him sometimes how he can paint yellow over blue and make green, and red over blue and make purple. Let him experiment.

Finger Painting – Finger paints can be bought at toy shops, and they are edible and water soluble so that you need not worry if some goes into his mouth. For this you will again need a smock or old shirt to cover up your child's clothes; and choose a spot where there is nothing to be spoiled. You will also need a washable table top or board, some blotting paper and a sponge and pots of finger paint.

Again, start with one colour. Damp the paper and smooth it down on the table top with the damp sponge and show your child how to drop a tiny piece of paint onto the paper and then to spread it and make patterns with his fingers. A bowl for washing his fingers should also be provided in a convenient place. When a picture is finished, it should be blotted and removed and fresh paper put down. Gradually show him how to use two colours and then three and how to mix them. Do not go on for too long. Pack up before he gets too tired or too wild. Do not worry too much about the mess at first, handling paints takes a lot of learning.

A handicapped child who is not yet standing can do this kind of painting.

It's his work – Make sure you do not curb your child's imagination and creativity by under-appreciating his efforts. There is more merit in a scribble or a crude drawing of a 'man' which your child has created entirely on his own than colouring in other people's pictures or drawing round templates. Show him techniques but leave him to apply them in his own way. Draw and paint with him but do not expect him to draw like you, or make him feel inferior.

Making a Scrap Book – It is important to respect your child's growing skill and imagination as soon as he starts to crayon or draw. Many parents put one or two of the best efforts up on the wall. Another way is to start a scrap book. You do not have to wait until he is drawing recognisable objects. He may be able to tell you what this drawing is meant to represent or if not you could suggest something. Small drawings can be cut out and stuck in. At first, you will have to do the cutting and sticking but you should let your child help with putting on the adhesive and also start getting the feel of using scissors. Although these prove difficult at first for the small fingers of Down's Syndrome children, they do learn to use them. You will probably have to do a lot of guiding at first. It is very instructive to watch a friend cutting a piece of paper or material with scissors. Note down all the different actions starting from picking the scissors up.

See which of these actions your child can do, then think how best you can help him with those actions he cannot do.

You can buy pairs of simple scissors from E.S.A. (see Fig. 25) which are much easier for children to use than ordinary scissors.

Paper Folding – It is second nature for us to be able to fold a sheet of paper in half neatly. At first a child finds this very

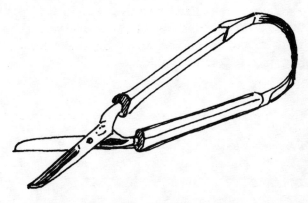

A pair of scissors for beginners

Fig. 25

hard. We can gain some insight into his difficulty if we take up origami! Make a beginning by showing your child how to make a small book by folding a page or two of paper. Let him staple it together. Put some little drawings in it and let him 'read' it or use it in doll play. Next, use some soft paper (a paper napkin will do) and show him how to fold this in four. Let him tear some holes in the folded napkin and then unfold it and see the pattern he has made. Make some mats like this for his party tea. If he is able to cut with scissors, show him how to cut out patterns. Interesting patterns can be made by putting a blob of paint in the middle of a sheet of paper and then folding it over firmly and leaving a while before unfolding the paper again.

SECTION 4: SOCIAL PLAY

Introduction

INTRODUCTION TO SOCIAL PLAY

It is important to be able to get on with other people. This is what a child learns to do when he is playing with other children. We call this social play. Toys, no matter how interesting or intriguing, cannot take the place of playing with brothers and sisters or friends.

Although social play can only occur when two or more people are present, social play is more than this. Just as you can be alone in a crowd, so too in a room full of children there may be no social play. Social play is only present when the children are interacting with each other.

Interacting

Interacting simply means that each person is responding to the other's actions; what one person does affects the other. It's rather like a conversation. If one person is doing all the talking and the other all the listening, that's not a conversation – that's a lecture! Likewise, it's not a conversation if both are talking at the same time – that's deafening! A conversation only occurs when the people take it in turns to speak and to listen. When they are conversing, they are interacting. Another way of thinking of interacting is in terms of 'give and take'. There is no interacting if one person is doing all the giving while the other is taking all he can get. Interacting involves both giving *and* taking; it's a *two-way* thing.

Social play

The basis of all social play activities is interaction between two people. Activities such as ball games, dominoes or playing shops require children to take turns and to give and take. If a person doesn't play his part, then the play cannot continue.

The origins of social play lie early in childhood. The earliest form of social play is play between parents and their children. Right from birth, the child is part of a social world filled with adults who can't resist playing with babies. This interaction is very enjoyable for both.

Social play between children develops later. Very young children rarely interact. If placed beside each other with a selection of toys, they will play just as though they were by themselves. They seem to be unaware of each other.

As they get older though, they start to notice what the other child is doing. They will even play with the toys in a similar way, copying each other. But they still are not interacting. It's just as if they were both talking at the same time, instead of conversing with each other.

Through time, children do start to engage in joint play activities. At first each seems more interested in his part, rather than in the other person. Gradually the children start to interact more. At this point, we could say that their social play has truly started.

Importance of social play
Social play is vital to all children's development, handicapped or not.

1. *Social play encourages children to learn from other people* – We learn a lot from watching and copying other people. The desire to do whatever they are doing is a big incentive to children's learning. Social play encourages the child to interact with other people and hence increases his opportunities to learn.

2. *Social play develops the child's ability to communicate* – Playing with another person requires you to be in 'communication' with that person. Thus through social play children can practise and extend their ability to communicate.

At first, they will use gestures, but later these will give way to language, the main means of communication in our society.

3. *Social play makes the child more sociable* – Young

children tend to be very self-centred and want things done their way. They don't take other people's desires into account. They can be totally selfish and hence very unsociable. This sort of behaviour may be all right in very young children, but if an older child behaves like this, adults call him 'spoilt' and other children, like as not, will refuse to play with him. But through social play, a child does learn to share and to take turns. He is then more likely to get on with other people, both adults and children.

4.   *Social play helps the child develop friendships* – Just think how important your friendships are to you. It is obvious then that we will want to encourage children to form their own friendships. Social play gives children the opportunity to do this. Through it they can learn the joys as well as the responsibilities of friendship.

Social play and the handicapped child

Obviously we will want to encourage all children's social play but with a handicapped child you may need to give it particular attention.

Play with adults – Earlier we said social play involved giving and taking. With a severely handicapped child, it is all too easy for us to do all the giving and never any taking. But this is *not* social play. We have to look out for ways in which he might be trying to give us a 'message'. He might screw his face up; make small grunts or shake his arms. Watch out for this sort of thing and respond to it; follow his lead.

Also give him time to respond to you. Sometimes we are so impatient that we rush onto something else and never give the child time to respond. So give him a chance to take part!

Play with children – A handicapped child will not have the same abilities as other children of the same age. Consequently, other children may be reluctant to play with the handicapped child, saying, 'He's too slow' or 'He messes around and spoils the game'.

To avoid this we need to help the handicapped child to learn to play with other children.

However, if the child is handicapped, we may be reluctant to let him play out with other children. But in doing this, we could be depriving the child of opportunities to develop social play. If the child is immobile or unable to move around easily, you can always invite other children in to play.

If the child has no brothers or sisters at home, or if they are much older, then we should make a special effort to ensure that the handicapped child does have opportunities to play with other children. Adult company is no substitute. If your child is under school-age, you may be able to arrange for him to attend a playgroup for some days a week. This will gradually get him used to being in the company of other children. Later on, he may be able to attend a nursery school before starting school proper. Your health visitor or social worker should be able to give you details of play-groups or nursery schools in your area.

Even when your child is attending school, you can still encourage him to mix with other children, for example, explore the possibility of him joining a youth organisation, such as the Boys' Brigade.

There is a lot you can do to encourage your child's social play. Later in this section we will be describing games and activities. But as we noted earlier, the nature of social play changes as the child develops. It is important therefore to pick activities which are suited to your child's level of development. If you pick activities which are too hard or too easy, your child will get no pleasure or benefit out of them. So before starting on any games, you need to find out your child's present level in social play. To help you do this we have prepared developmental charts.

Developmental Charts
You should find the charts useful in three ways:
1. *The charts show the stages children go through in social play* – The items have been arranged in the order children usually develop them; the earliest activity is given first and the most advanced last. Thus as you read down the page, you

will see the stages in the development of children's social play.

2. *The charts give you a framework for observing your child* – The charts highlight specific activities which show the development of social play. Observe your child playing with an adult and other children and see which of the activities he can do and which he can't. By doing this you will learn more about your child's present level of development.

3. *The charts provide a means of recording your child's progress* – Beside each item you can record whether your child can (tick YES) or cannot (tick NO) do that item. If you go through the charts at regular intervals, say every six months (marking the items with different coloured pens on each occasion), you will be able to record his progress in social play. This will be a great source of encouragement to you.

We suggest that you now read through the charts. Then over the next few days observe your child and record whether he does any of the items listed. Once you have done this, we can then guide you to suitable games and activities for your child.

Choosing play activities

We have grouped the social play games and activities in three booklets:

Booklet 1, *Play with Me*, is concerned with the early forms of social play, particularly that between parent and child.

Booklet 2, *Two of Us*, describes activities requiring at least two people, either adult and child, or two children.

Booklet 3, *Taking Turns*, extends these activities into games with rules.

You will have noticed the titles of the booklets listed alongside the items in the charts. Look back at the charts; if you have ticked NO to any of the items covered by the first booklet, then we suggest you go first to Booklet 1 (p. 147) and try some of the activities given there.

If the first item you ticked NO is covered by Booklet 2; then we suggest you look at that booklet first (see p. 155), and leave out Booklet 1.

Social Play Charts

Enjoys being swung, lifted in play etc.	YES	NO	
Enjoys peek-a-boo	YES	NO	
Joins in games of clap-hands and pat-a-cake	YES	NO	*Booklet 1 Play with me p. 147*
Offers a toy to an adult and gives it when requested	YES	NO	

Begins to co-operate in play with other children – shares his toys etc	YES	NO	
Copies other children's play activities although the children do not play together	YES	NO	*Booklet 2 Two of us p. 155*
Plays co-operatively with one other child; takes turns in games such as play-shop etc.	YES	NO	

Plays co-operatively in a group of children in games such as hide-and-seek, ball games etc.	YES	NO	
Enters into the spirit of race games	YES	NO	*Booklet 3 Taking turns p. 164*
Plays correctly games with simple rules (e.g. snap, dominoes) – keeps to rules, awaits turn	YES	NO	

If the first item you ticked NO is covered by Booklet 3, or if you ticked all the items YES, then look at Booklet 3 first (p. 164) and leave out Booklets 1 and 2.

Once you start the games, note carefully your child's reaction. If he makes no attempt to join in, then you could be expecting too much of him. Try some 'simpler' activities. On the other hand, if he joins in readily but soon stops, it could be that the game is too easy and he's bored. Try some more 'advanced' activities.

BOOKLET 1: PLAY WITH ME

All the activities in this booklet are centred around a young child's favourite toy – his Mum or Dad. It's easy to see why they are his favourite. What other toy can make lots of different noises, change appearance, lift and rock you and fetch you things you want? For the young child, no other toy can possibly replace his parents.

Yet the play between parent and child is so natural that we tend to overlook its importance. The relationship which a child forms with his parents is the foundation for all his future relationships. It will also improve his confidence in all aspects of learning and development. A child who has a strong, secure relationship with his parents is much more likely to develop close relationships with others than the child who hasn't.

Also important is how the parents get on with other adults and children. Children often model themselves on their parents. If his parents are rather domineering, then he too is likely to be domineering.

Thus, parents are by far the child's most valuable toy.

Learning to play with parents

But the child has to learn to play with his 'toy'. Indeed at first, it's the parent who seems to do most of the 'playing', the child seemingly content to watch. But this is valuable experience for the child and a great incentive for him to join in. Gradually he will become more responsive and an active partner in the games. Of course, this encourages parents to play all the more with the child; they enjoy it as much as he does!

Not all children develop social play as easily as this suggests. Some handicapped children may be very unresponsive. They may rarely react to people. Consequently, parents get no encouragement to play with their child. It is all too easy then to spend less and less time playing. But this will only encourage the child to remain unresponsive, for now he will have nobody to respond to! With these children it is important to establish a play routine. However much you play with your child in the course of everyday activities you should also set aside at least ten minutes a day for playing with your child. Pick a time when your child is alert and comfortable and you are unlikely to be disturbed. You can concentrate solely on him.

Your aim in these sessions is to encourage your child to become an active partner in all the games. Here are some points to bear in mind:

Give him time to take part – During the games, pause as though you were expecting him to respond. Rather like in a conversation; say your bit and wait for him to reply. At first you may get nothing, but you are giving him a chance which through time he will take up. Incidentally, you may need to have a fairly long pause, for some children can take a while to respond.

Watch out for odd responses – Children sometimes respond in a way which we did not expect of them. Watch carefully what your child does; it might be a very small movement of the hand or head; a soft grunt etc. Often we call children 'unresponsive' when in fact it is simply us being 'unobservant' and not spotting their responses.

Follow their lead – As adults we are so used to deciding things for children that even at playtime we decide how the games will be played. We want things done our way. Instead give them a chance to lead while you follow them. You will be surprised how much children can blossom out when this happens.

Activities which you could use at these playtimes are described below. Many of them will be very familiar to you, for they are activities which adults spontaneously use with babies and young children. They are equally suitable for severely handicapped children of all ages.

Cuddles – Young babies tend to be cuddled a lot by their parents. Not so older children, except perhaps when they are tired or frightened. It is important to continue cuddling the handicapped child. This provides the child with a direct experience of social play. He can 'concentrate' on his parent's face, voice and experience rocking movements, etc. When he's that close to his Mum or Dad, there is not much to distract him. Don't just cuddle him when he's tired; make it part of all your play sessions.

With children who have problems in hearing or seeing, it is particularly important that you encourage their sense of touch. Cuddling is especially good for them.

Action Songs – Again, these can be particularly helpful for children who have either sensory difficulties or movement difficulties or both. If you repeat an action song such as 'Round and round the garden, like a teddy bear!' on regular occasions with your child, he will came to recognise the action sequence. This is both enjoyable and reassuring to a young child, because familiarity helps a child to make sense of his world. He will also have his part to play, however slightly, such as tensing up in anticipation before you 'tickle him under there'.

Tickling – You may have to do a bit of exploring to find your child's 'sensitive' areas. They may be under the chin, soles of the feet, palms of the hands, under the arms etc. As you try each of these, see if he reacts by squirming, trying to move away etc. You can use his 'tickling' area in rhymes such as 'Round and round the garden'.

Once he starts smiling and laughing, he becomes much more sociable and you get a lot more fun too!

All Change – As you talk to him, change your tone of voice. Your child is much more likely to take notice of the *way* you say things rather than what you say. You can talk higher or deeper, soft or loud, slow or fast, or even burst into song, but do it gradually. If you change suddenly, you could frighten him. Variety of voice will make you a more interesting person to listen to.

Similarly you can vary your facial expression when playing with your child. Exaggerate your mouth movements and raise your eyebrows; you can look surprised, or smile or frown etc.

Also wearing different hats or ear-rings or glasses will encourage the child to look at you. Even holding objects in your mouth for him to grasp focuses attention on you at the same time!

Finally, as you 'talk' to your child, don't remain in the one position; move around. This will encourage him to become more active, in that he will follow you with his eyes or turn his head, as you move around.

Rough and Tumble – Being lifted and swung around can be a great source of stimulation for handicapped children. One reason is that it brings them into close contact with their parents. Although it can be very tiring, it is worth having a short session each day. It will also help the child's physical development (see *Energetic Play* section, p. 84).

During the rough and tumble you can suddenly 'freeze'. Do nothing, until your child makes a move. At first it might only be a slight movement of the arms or legs but you can take this as a sign that he wants the game to continue. These pauses will let the child know that he has a part to play in this game. In time he will let you know what he wants to do.

Peek-a-boo – There are many variations of peek-a-boo. In the simplest version, all you need to do is cover your face with your hands when your child is watching you. Then move them away quickly and as you do, start talking. On other occasions, instead of opening your hands, peep round the side or over the top of them. This will be an extra surprise.

Alternatively, if your child is in his pram or cot, all you do is 'disappear' by kneeling down and suddenly 'popping' back into view.

Another version requires the child to be rather more active. This time you hide behind a cloth (handkerchief, headscarf etc.) and your child has to pull it away to find you. At first he might need some help from another person, e.g. Mum can show him what to do while Dad hides. At first, drop the cloth as soon as he touches it. Then gradually increase your demands, until he will pull it away from your head. Similarly you can play peek-a-boo with him. That is, you can cover his face with the cloth and either he or you, can pull it off.

Hide-away – This game follows on from the other peek-a-boo game, and is especially suitable for children who are mobile. Here, Mum or Dad hides behind a curtain or settee or door etc. and the child has to find them. When first playing the game, you may need to look out several times to remind him that you are there. Later he should be able to find you if you keep calling him, and even without you saying anything.

To give him the idea of hiding, one of you (e.g. Mum) can 'hide' with your child, while Dad 'searches' for you. This game is an early version of hide-and-seek.

Copy-cats – Children learn a great deal from copying their parents and this is something we should encourage them to do. One of the best ways to do this, is for you to copy them; you do whatever they do, shaking head, making noises, waving hands etc. Seeing you will encourage him to continue, and soon you won't know who is copying who! This sort of game you can play almost anywhere or at any time. The nice thing about it is that the child is in 'charge'; he decides the action and you follow him.

Later, you can start to play a more active part. Now as well as copying the child's action, you change it slightly perhaps by adding on another part. For example, if your child is saying 'da-da-da-da' you can start to say 'da-da-da-*dee*' (emphasise the last part) or if he is waving his arm, you end the action by banging on an object (table, ball etc.). This will help him to learn new things.

Lend a hand – Some children may need special help to encourage them to copy. Here's an idea you could use. One parent (e.g. Dad) sits behind the child, while Mum is facing him. Mum then does an action which you have seen the child do before, e.g. hits a tin with hand. At the same time, Dad then 'prompts' the child to do this action. He takes the child's arm and makes the child hit the tin. Make a great fuss as the child does it. As you practise this, Dad can give the child less help so that he has to do the copying on his own. Each time you introduce a new action, prompt him at the beginning.

Mirror – Mirrors are often a great incentive for a child to make lots of actions. A full length mirror is particularly useful; ideally one that goes down to the floor so that your child can sit in front of it. If you sit with him, he will see you and himself do the actions.

Nursery Rhymes – Nursery rhymes or songs with actions can be very good for encouraging the child to copy you. Although he may not be able to say or sing the rhymes, at least he can take part by doing the actions. You should start with fairly simple rhymes in which there is only one action, e.g. 'Little Jack Horner' (pull out thumb) or 'Ring-a-Ring-a-Roses' (all fall down). As your child learns these, you can introduce rhymes with a variety of actions, e.g. 'This is the way we wash our clothes' (...comb our hair etc.) or 'The Wheels on the Bus'.

Looking at books – Children can learn so much from looking at books with you that it is well worthwhile putting aside a few minutes each day for doing just this. And it is not so much the learning from books that is important but learning from you. The book is merely a focus for you both. The child knows he has your attention and if you are cuddling him on your knee, he can hear all you say and see all the things you do. He can play his part, e.g. turning the pages, while you tell the story. This activity, perhaps more than any other, will help your child to feel really close to you. (For more details on books, see *Imaginative Play* section, p. 197).

Roll-a-ball – Young children are often reluctant to part with toys. They hold onto them until they drop or lose interest in them. This game gets children used to the idea that you don't need to hold onto toys in order to 'play' with them. All you do is simply sit your child on the floor (with back supported as necessary), legs slightly apart. You sit facing him a little distance away and roll the ball to him. (The ball shouldn't be so big that he finds it difficult to hold nor so small that he has difficulty finding it.) The idea is for you to roll the ball back and forwards to each other. At first your child will probably 'drop' the ball by accident rather than intentionally roll it to you. However, act as though he has done his part and roll the ball back to him. Make a great fuss as he drops the ball and when you roll it back, but say nothing if he's holding onto it (he's ignoring you, so you ignore him!). Gradually he will start to roll or kick the ball back to you. This activity will lead into the throwing, and kicking games we will be describing in Booklet 2 (p. 155).

Swap you – Young children don't understand the idea of giving. What they have, they hold onto. They don't want to share. Here is a game that will encourage them to give.

Collect some toys and give him one to play with. After a moment or two, hold out another toy and as he reaches for it, hold out your other hand, ready to take back the toy which the child has. At first you probably will need to take the toy from him; he won't give it to you, but in time he will get the idea of swapping.

Give-me game – Another version of the above game is the following. Have the child sitting up, either at a table or a chair with a tray on it. Collect together several of the child's favourite toys.

Place one of these on the table, then holding out your hand say 'Give me'. It is unlikely that your child will do this, so you will need another person to prompt the child, by taking his hand, lifting the toy and giving it to you. Now for the important part; as the child has given you his toy, you need to give him something in return. The best thing to use is something you know he really likes – ice-cream, jelly, chocolate, drink of milk etc. But only give very small amounts at a time. As soon as the child gives you the toy, straight away give him his reward.

Gradually you will be able to stop prompting him, so that when the toy is placed in front of him and you say 'Give me', he hands it to you. Later on you can place down a number of toys and he has to hand them all to you before he has the reward.

You might also find that you no longer need to give the child sweets etc. Just saying 'Good boy' or smiling etc. is enough.

Remember also, to give your child a chance to *ask* for the objects, while you do the giving. Take it in turns to ask for, and to give each other, the objects.

Learning Language – We said earlier that parents are by far the child's most valuable toy. This is especially so when it comes to helping the child learn language. No other toy will ever be able to do this. Our book, *Let Me Speak*, will give you lots of ideas for games you can play with your child to help him learn language.

BOOKLET 2: TWO OF US

The games and activities in this booklet all require at least two people. They can be used to extend the social play between parents and their child (dealt with in Booklet 1, see p. 147) or you can use them to encourage social play between two children.

Giving in

We noted earlier that young children are often reluctant to play together. They don't want to share their toys and want to do things their own way. There is a danger with handicapped children that we encourage them to continue to act like this. We always give in to them and don't make them share. Often it's relatives and friends who are inclined to do this rather than the parents. Yet it is false kindness. We are depriving the child of learning to play with others.

Practising with parents

The activities in this booklet are designed to help the child learn to play with other people, especially other children. But first the child needs to practise the activity with his parents. Mum or Dad takes the part of the other child. In this way, the child learns what is expected of him and is better prepared to cope with the more demanding situation of playing with another child. However, it is important for the parents to play their part properly. Make sure the child does take his turn. Don't give in to him too easily. If he spoils the game by messing around or opting out, just pack the things away. Don't coax him back. Other children won't; they will just ignore him. So in these games, you may need to be fairly 'tough' with him; at least as 'tough' as other children will be with him.

Meeting other children

It is important that the child does have an opportunity to play with other children. Younger brothers and sisters can be a great help to the handicapped child. Although you have to be careful to make playing with the handicapped child an enjoyable experience for them and not an obligation.

If the child has no young brothers or sisters, perhaps he could play with neighbours' children. You can invite them into your house.

Generally speaking, handicapped children can play better with younger children for their abilities are more alike. Nevertheless, in some activities the handicapped child may well be able to play with children of the same age. You can't make hard and fast rules. Simply let him experience playing with children of different ages and see which works out best.

Getting used to other children

You will need to help your child get used to the idea of playing with other children. The first stage in this, is a simple extension of the games you and he have been playing. That is, instead of just the two of you, bring in another child. You now play with each child turn about. For example, in the Roll-a-ball game (p. 152), you would roll the ball to one and when he rolls it back, you then roll the ball to the other child.

Although the children are not playing together, they are getting used to each other. They will be watching what the other is doing and it will also give them the idea of taking turns.

When you think about it, this is a very obvious thing to do and yet when two children get together, adults tend to leave them to play instead of joining in with them. Many of the activities in Booklet 1 (p. 147) can be used, or here are some others:

Pass the parcel – Prepare the parcel by wrapping a toy or

sweet in a sheet of paper. Then wrap this parcel with another toy or sweet in another sheet of paper, forming a bigger parcel. Continue doing this until you have a whole lot of parcels inside each other.

The children then take it in turns to unwrap the parcel. Each time they remove a sheet of paper, they find another parcel, which they pass onto the other child, and a toy or sweet, which they keep. Your job is to make sure that they do take turns!

Towers of bricks – Give the children an equal number of bricks but instead of each one building a tower, get them to take turns at putting a brick on the same tower, thereby making a giant tower. They can also take it in turns to knock it down!

Encouraging them to play together
The next step is to start getting them to play together without you having to direct operations. To do this, you should choose the activity carefully. There are three points to bear in mind:
1. The activity should definitely require two people. One person should not be able to do it by himself, or at least, not very satisfactorily.
2. Both children should be active all the time. One should not have to wait and watch, while the other plays.
3. The child should be capable of the action or actions required by the game. Children often stop playing together because one cannot do the action. You therefore need to choose simple activities.

Here are some examples of activities you could use to start getting children to play together.

See-Saw – This is an excellent early activity. You can buy one; or improvise your own or else use the one in the playground. A word of warning though; some handicapped children may feel very insecure on a see-saw. You might need to give them additional support at their back and sides.

Tug-of-War – The traditional tug-of-war game of trying to

pull a person (or team) over a line may not be very attractive to young children. (However, older children may delight in it, especially if a group of them are trying to pull an adult over!)

For the younger child you can retain the basic idea in a game such as the following.

Crackers – Pulling a Christmas cracker requires two people and if each gets a 'prize' it is worth while taking part. However, crackers can be rather expensive, so you might like to make your own. You can do this out of newspaper. Loosely roll up a sheet of newspaper. Place inside two identical 'prizes' (sweets, small toys etc.). Twist the ends of the roll and you've got a cracker. It doesn't 'bang' but the children will probably not care as they will have the satisfaction of breaking it open and getting a prize!

Incidentally, the more tightly you roll the newspaper, the harder it will be for them to break it. Beware of doing it so tightly that it is impossible to break – even by adults.

Pull apart – This is basically a re-usable 'cracker'. Simply saw a broom-stick in half and then rejoin the pieces using a metal or plastic collar (a short length of piping will do). The important thing is to have a really tight fit, so that it takes a bit of effort to pull the sticks apart. This can then be used as a 'cracker' – the children having to pull the ends to get at the 'prize' which you can put into the piping.

Chute – A chute made out of cardboard tube or plastic drain piping can be a good social play activity. It works best if you can have the chute supported in the middle so that it can be moved up and down (like a see-saw). A piece of string firmly tied in the middle will do (see Fig. 26). One child can then 'post' an object to the other. He then moves his end of the chute up, to post an object back.

Another use of the chute is to encourage children to talk to each other, for with the tube their voices will be amplified. They can take turns at talking and listening.

Push-carts – These can provide a good focus for social play. You can either buy them or else make your own out of a

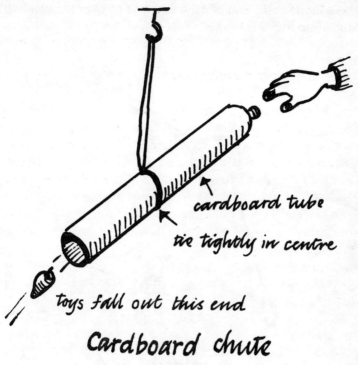

cardboard tube

tie tightly in centre

toys fall out this end

Cardboard chute

Fig. 26

wooden box, broom handles and a pair of wheels or use a wheel barrow. The fun can be both in riding in the car or pushing it and children may need to be encouraged to share if they have a distinct preference for one or the other. Nevertheless, they can develop the activity by introducing an imaginative element, e.g. pretending to be a bus; one person the driver, the other a conductor with other children as passengers (if there's room!).

Flying ball – The idea of this game is that a ball moves backward and forward along pieces of string held by two children. It works as follows – You need to have *two* long pieces of string (12 ft or more) and a ball (or other object) with a small hole through it. Galt's make hard plastic balls like this. You thread both pieces of string through the ball.

Make loops at the end of each string to go over the children's hands (see Fig. 27).

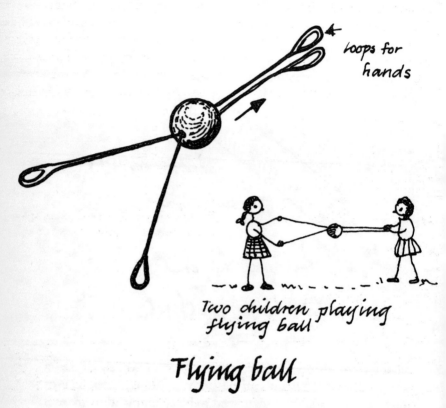

loops for hands

Two children playing flying ball

Flying ball

Fig. 27

Have the children face each other and far enough apart to make the string tight. When one of the children opens his arms wide, the ball will fly down the strings to the other child. Then when he opens his arms, the ball will go back again. (That is when the other child puts his hands together.) The children really do have to co-operate to make the ball go back and forth.

Ball games – These are as much social play as they are energetic play. Ball games are much more satisfactory if two or more are playing. Hence you should encourage children's ability to kick, throw and catch balls, for it will mean that a whole new range of social play activities is open to them. In the section on energetic play we have suggestions for doing this (see p. 93).

As an introduction to 'team' games such as football, rounders etc. it is good to encourage two children to play together in simple games such as kicking or throwing the ball backwards and forwards to each other; or scoring goals with one as the goal-keeper and the other the kicker. Harder games such as catching or hitting the ball with a bat can be introduced later.

Often these games are sufficient in themselves to keep the child's interest. If necessary though, you can introduce an element of competition by chalking up a point for each 'goal' or catch or ball hit by the bat. The child gets a prize depending on the number of points he has.

Three-legged race – This activity rather forces children to play together, and it can be very difficult and even distressing for young children. However, you can get the same effect by simply tying them together at the waist (leave 2 or 3 feet of rope between them), or by 'hand-cuffing' them together. The children can then act as a team in race games or ball games, maybe playing 'against' an adult.

All play can be social play

Up to now we have been describing activities which really do need two people. In a sense we have been 'forcing' the children to play together, for the activity can only continue if both take part.

However, we should be encouraging children to play together in other activities; even ones which they could play by themselves. Many imaginative play activities are particularly suited to getting children playing together (see *Imaginative Play* section, p. 177).

But even in activities like drawing, building towers, jigsaws etc. you can encourage them to work together.

To help them do this, you may need to arrange the situations so that they need to co-operate. Here are some examples:

Match-box towers – Match-boxes make very good building units. All you need to do is glue the trays of *two* match-boxes into one lid (see Fig. 28). These we will call the 'big

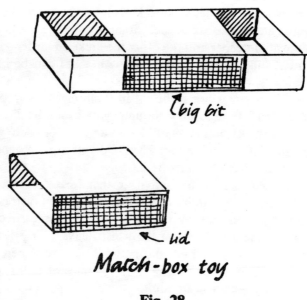

'big bit

lid

Match-box toy

Fig. 28

bits'. For every big bit, you will have a spare lid. By slotting the big bits into the lid, you can build up a tower or make a wall (if the boxes are placed on their sides) or make a train (if placed flat).

Of course, a child could do all this by himself. But if you give one child all the big bits and the other the spare lids, then they will have to share, if they want to build anything. Each will contribute to the final product.

Drawing – Have a large sheet of paper, big enough for both children to draw on without getting in each other's way. You can then draw in the outline of the scene: house, tree, car etc.

and allocate parts for them to colour in. Alternatively, they can 'agree' to draw a particular scene: each doing different parts. Either way, the finished picture is the work of both.

Threading game – Two children can work with the same length of string; threading beads on at each end. If one child lets go, then all the beads will fall off!

With a bit of thought, most activities can be arranged so that the children will need to co-operate more.

Group of children

Once your child can play happily with one other child, you can gradually introduce him to a group of children playing the same or similar activities. Later, you can introduce activities which are designed more for a group rather than just two people. We will be describing some of these in Booklet 3 (p. 164).

BOOKLET 3: TAKING TURNS

This booklet is concerned with more advanced social play activities; that is, those requiring a group of people. This includes team games such as football, rounders and cricket or indoor games such as ludo, dominoes etc. Of course, these activities are not confined to childhood; they can be enjoyed at all ages.

If your child enjoys some of the games outlined in this chapter, we suggest you might like to have a look at another book in the Human Horizons series, *Let's Join In*. This book is full of suggestions which will help youngsters to join in with others on equal terms in games and recreations and integrate with their own age group. Another book in this series, *Let Me Count*, describes games which help to develop early mathematical skills and understanding.

Importance for the handicapped child

It is very important that we encourage handicapped children to learn to take part in these activities. There are two reasons:

1. *Family* – These activities are ones which the whole family can join in. By taking part in them, the handicapped child will become a fuller member of the family. There are many other ways in which you can do this, for example by giving him a job to do at home – emptying the waste basket, making the beds. The particular job can vary according to his abilities but whatever it is, he is responsible for that job.

2. *Leisure* – It will help him to develop 'leisure' interests. This is particularly important for after school. Handicapped young people can become increasingly house-bound as they get older.

Furthermore, if they can take part in these leisure activities, they will have the opportunity to mix with non-handicapped people. Keep a look out for the sort of activities the young people in your area do. They may well have changed since your youth!

Of course, some handicapped children will have a specific disability which will prevent them from taking part in these activities, especially the more energetic ones, like football. However, many children don't take part simply because they don't understand the rules. This is where they need you to help them. In this booklet we will be describing ways in which you can make it easier for children to learn the rules of the games.

Learning the rules – Part 1
It is very difficult to learn the rules of a game while it is being played. There is so much going on. You need to make the situation simpler. You can follow this plan:
1. *Parent and Child* – First of all, play the game with only you and your child. This will give you a chance to introduce him to the rules gradually. A word of warning though: don't always let your child win. Remember he has to learn to lose as well!
2. *Two Children* – Once the child has mastered some of the basic rules you can let him play the game with another child. You will need to act as 'referee' though, for there could well be some cheating or disputes.
3. *Group of Children* – As the child increases his ability to play the game properly, you can introduce more people; either other members of the family, or other children. The more people, the longer each person has to wait to take part, so watch out for signs of impatience. If some of the children are much better than others, give them a handicap, e.g. in darts they have to stand further away.

Indeed, we have been using this plan in this section; Booklet 1 (see p. 147), dealing with Parents and Child, and Booklet 2 (see p. 155), dealing with two children.

However, this plan will only help the children to cope with the number of people playing the game. Within each 'stage' you will need to help them learn the rules.

Learning the Rules – Part 2

When you think of it, some of our so-called simple games have quite a number of rules that have to be followed if the game is to be played properly. If you introduce these all at once, it will be very hard for the child to remember them. And more difficult to understand them. You should aim to introduce the rules one at a time. Here is an example of how you can do this for the game 'Snakes and Ladders'. But you can use the same approach with any game.

List the rules – First make a list of all the rules in the game. For Snakes and Ladders these are:

1. Move your man from the starting point to the finishing point.
2. Move along the number of places indicated by the dice:
   If it shows 1, move 1 square
   If it shows 2, move 2 squares and so on
   (In all there are six rules here.)
3. Take turns to throw the dice.
4. If you land on a square with the bottom of a ladder on it, move your man to the top of the ladder.
5. If you land on a square with the head of a snake on it, you drop down the snake.
6. First man to reach the finishing point is the winner.

These are the basic rules of this game. Other versions may have additional rules, e.g. 'Throw a six to start' or 'Follow instructions written in the square you land in, e.g. "Go forward three squares"'. But we will concentrate on the basic rules.

Simplify the game – It will be difficult for children to grasp all the rules at once. So we can simplify the game by leaving out some rules and concentrating on the others. For example, you could concentrate on rules 1, 2 and 3 above. The game would then be a simple race game, rather like this:

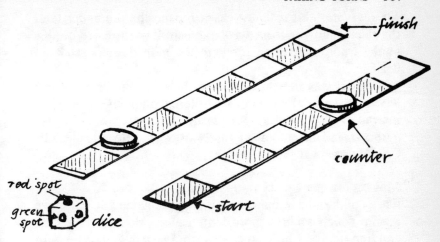

Race game with dice

Fig. 29

Race Game – You need two strips of card divided into squares as shown in Fig. 29. At first, have only about 10 squares. You will need a special dice. One which has a red spot on three sides and a green spot on the other three. (You can stick gummed paper over the numbers on an ordinary dice.) When the dice is thrown, and green is uppermost, you can move forward one space. But if red shows, you don't move.

As an incentive you can place a 'prize' (sweet etc.) at each finishing point, so that once his man lands there the child gets the prize.

You take it in turns to throw the dice, moving your man towards the finish. However, in this game there is a prize for both.

Reasons for the changes – You may find this game is nothing like snakes and ladders, but there are good reasons for the changes:

10 squares: This ensures that the game doesn't last too long and reduces the danger of the child losing interest.

Straight-line: This makes it easier for the child to understand the rule of moving from start to finish. It is harder to do this in the traditional game for here the path doubles back on itself.

Dice: This gets the child used to throwing the dice without having to worry about what the different numbers mean. Thus instead of the six rules noted earlier, there are just two.

Two strips: This eliminates the 'winner' and 'loser' rule. The child always 'wins'.

Making the game more complicated

Once children have mastered this simple game you can have a game which is a little more complicated. Alternatively, some children may not need to have such a simple game and with them you could start with a more complicated version. You can increase the complexity of the game by

(a) Having a longer course, e.g. increase the number of squares to 20 or 30 etc.

(b) Varying the shape of the course. Make it double back on itself.

This increases the complexity of the game without introducing any new rules. However, once the child is keeping to the rules and waiting for his turn etc., you can then start to introduce a new rule into the game.

New Rules

Winner – For example, we could decide to introduce Rule 6 'The first man to reach the finishing point is the winner'.

Now, instead of two strips, you have only one. Both men move along this; 'racing' to get the prize. If you win, you keep the prize. Don't give it to your child even if he obviously wants it. If you do, he won't learn the rule!

Dice – Or we could introduce some of the rules with the dice. For example, replace all the 'red' sides of the dice with green, but on three green sides draw 1 black dot and on the other three, 2 black dots. Now the child can move forward one or two squares according to the throw of the dice.

Once he has grasped the idea of 'two' squares you can introduce 3 dots, then 4 dots, and so on, until he can play with an ordinary dice. However, it may be difficult for the child to grasp the difference in the numbers and count them for himself. So don't wait until he knows all these rules. Go on and introduce the other rules of the game, using the simpler dice.

Ladders – It is better to introduce these before the snakes as they let players get to the prize sooner. Introduce quite a number so that the child has lots of opportunities to go up the ladder (see Fig. 30).

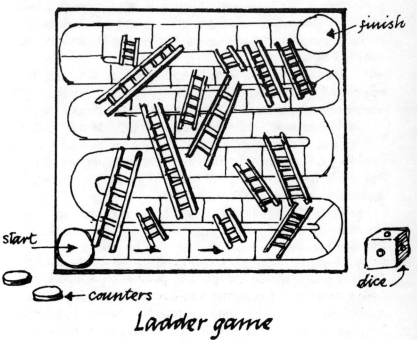

Ladder game

Fig. 30

Snakes – When your child has got the idea of the ladders, you can then add the snakes. Again, have quite a number to let him get the idea; there will always be the ladders to help the child get back up!

By now the child will be able to play a recognisable game of snakes and ladders, although the dice may still be rather odd, in that it might have only three numbers on it. However, he can continue to 'learn' the dice as he plays the game or any other which requires dice, e.g. Ludo.

Other Games

You can use exactly the same approach with any other games – Ludo, dominoes, darts, rounders, football etc. With a bit of thought you can start off from a much simpler version. To help you we have given brief descriptions of some simpler games below. We leave it up to you to decide how you can introduce other rules and make it more like the 'real thing'. But remember to do this *gradually*, just as we did in the 'snakes and ladders' example.

NOTE: Although we call these 'simple' versions, they can still be enjoyed by the whole family, or a group of children. You don't need to wait until the child can play the proper game.

Simple Dominoes – It is much easier for children to match colours than numbers of dots. So replace the numbers with colours. You can easily do this using coloured gummed paper. But at first have only three colours. Five dominoes per player is probably enough at the beginning.

The basic idea is still the same. Players take it in turns to place down a domino which matches one already on the table. The first person to get rid of all his dominoes is the winner.

Simple Darts – Although real darts are rather dangerous, children can be introduced to the game by using darts fitted with rubber suction pads. These darts are fired from a 'gun' and will stick onto a board. Most toy shops sell these. The simplest game is one of just trying to get the darts to hit and stick on the board. At first, let the child stand fairly close to the board. Keep a count of the number of times he gets a dart in. The winner can be the first person to get 5 (or 10 or 15) darts in. As usual, players take turns to throw the darts. (To make it more interesting, draw a funny face as a target with one extra point for hitting the nose!)

Once the child can hit the board consistently from a reasonable distance (6 feet plus), you can introduce a more difficult version. This time cover the dart board with a sheet of paper with a large coloured circle in its middle. Now the child scores five points if he gets his dart in the middle (the bull's eye), and one point if he hits the outer area.

Later on, you can divide the board into four parts (see Fig. 31) then eight etc. A dart in each part scores a different

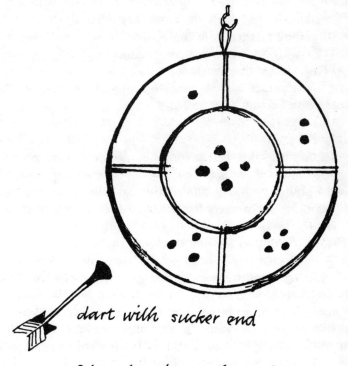

dart with sucker end

Simple dart-board

Fig. 31

number of points. As you may by now have realised, darts can be an entertaining way of helping the child learn to count! (It's best to use dots rather than numbers at the beginning. The child can then see whether he has scored more than the other players.)

Handicaps

In darts, and indeed in any other game, you can make the competition fairer by handicapping the more able players. This means that they can enjoy the game too and that they don't have to deliberately ease up to let the less able child win.

Some handicaps which you could use in darts are:

(a) Standing further from the board
(b) Throwing with non-preferred hand
(c) Throwing with eyes closed.

NOTE: Card games such as snap, happy families etc. will be discussed in Section 6: *Puzzle-it-out Play* (p. 230).

Outdoor Games

With outdoor games such as football, rounders or cricket, the rules of the game are *not* the most important thing. Rather, it is the ability to do the different things which are required. For example, in rounders the child needs to be able to:

1. Hit the ball with a bat
2. Bowl (or throw) the ball to the batsman
3. 'Field' the ball and throw to the batsman.

The child will need to practise doing all these with an adult only (see Booklet 2, p. 155). When he has grasped what is required, you can introduce him to the 'team' situation. You can still simplify the game though. For example, by having him run to a single point and back, rather than round in a circle. Or by letting him use a large bat.

You can handicap the other players by making them run further, use a small bat etc.

There is a wide variety of games which you can use, some more complicated than others. Here's a short list just to remind you, but you will probably be able to think of others:

Bat and Ball games – Rounders, cricket, tennis, badminton, putting and golf.

Ball games – These are team games like football, rugby. Or group games such as *Donkey* or *Pig in the Middle* – two people throw the ball to each other while the third person tries to get it. If he does, one of them becomes the 'pig'.

Chasing games – There are lots of variations here, e.g. *Stick in the mud* – when you are caught by the catcher you stand still on the spot where you were caught. However, another player, still at large, can free you by shaking hands with you. The game ends when all the players are stuck! Another good chasing game is hide-and-seek.

Race games – Again there are lots of variations, e.g. sack races, wheel-barrow races, three-legged race (but see p. 161).

Jumping games – Long jump or high jump. These are especially good as beach activities. Also *Hopscotch* and *Skipping* – two children hold the rope while the others skip.

Quoits – You can simplify this in much the same way as darts (see p. 170).

Skittles – Keep a score of the number each person knocks over.

Party games – There are plenty of books about party games, so we are not going to describe any here. It's worth looking through some of these books (in the library maybe) for they will give you lots of ideas for interesting and novel games the whole family can join in.

NOTE: Details of how to adapt games for physically handicapped children can be obtained from the Spastics Society (see p. 250).

SECTION 5: IMAGINATIVE PLAY

INTRODUCTION TO IMAGINATIVE PLAY

The essence of childhood is captured in a child's play. At the very heart of this play lies the world of make-believe, pretence and imagination. Here a child creates his own world around everyday objects and toys. He 'pretends' to feed his doll with food which is not there, or to drive a car along an imaginary roadway!

Some children develop very 'vivid imaginations': pebbles are transformed into people, bears are imagined peering between the cracks on the pavement and so on.

What is it about this kind of play which distinguishes it from other kinds of play?

In imaginative play a child is always adding something to the situation. He is picturing or imagining something that is not *really* there; in feeding a doll there is no *real* food and certainly the dolls cannot *really* eat it.

In make-believe a child is using objects or gestures to 'stand for' something else or as a sign or *symbol* of something else. A box can be used as a symbol of a car, a sucking noise can be a symbol of a teddy-bear eating ice-cream, and so on. This is why imaginative play is sometimes called symbolic play.

The beginnings of imaginative play

A child is not born being able to pretend or make-believe. This ability develops gradually in stages. At first the young baby is a little materialist; he is only interested in discovering what the 'real' world is like. So he treats all his toys alike – shakes, drops, smells, bites, examines and listens to them.

Only later will he start to treat each toy differently and 'roll' the ball or 'shake' the rattle, and so on.

The beginning of 'pretence' play comes a little later and may be very fleeting and hard to spot. It may consist of a swift dab with a spoon at a doll's mouth or a fumbling 'drink' from a toy cup.

But it is from such humble beginnings that elaborate games like 'Cowboys and Indians' later develop.

The importance of imaginative play

It is fun to watch children's 'make-believe' play, but is it important? After all, we may think that life is concerned with reality and only artists, poets, actors and such like need this kind of imagination in later life.

This argument may sound fair enough, but it is wrong.

1. *Imaginative play helps to develop thought and language* – The ability to *add* something to the situation; to picture it, or to allow one object or action to *stand* for another is absolutely essential for a developing human being.

For the dawn of imagination is also the dawn of our *mental ability*. Thought is not possible without the ability to imagine or 'picture' in your mind things which are not present.

The same is true of language. That same ability to pretend, or picture things which are not there, is essential for language development. A child cannot ask for something out of the cupboard unless he can imagine or 'picture it' when it is not there. 'Out of sight, out of mind' is all too true of the very young or immature child.

In play, children learn to use and recognise signs and symbols. They understand symbolic gestures in games like 'Round and round the garden'. This helps them later to learn to recognise other accepted sound-symbols which we call *words*

The symbolic 'barking' of a dog or 'mooing' of a cow in play eventually becomes an ability to use the proper words to convey ideas.

2. *Imaginative play helps children to understand others* – However, imagination is not only important in childhood.

Grown-ups need to be able to use their imagination too, if they are to understand others. They must be able to put themselves in another's place. This is what children are learning to do in playing mothers and fathers, or hospitals.

3.   *Imaginative play encourages creativity* – The person who is blessed with an imagination is likely to be inventive in all everyday situations; for instance, in discerning what is wrong with the car, in inventing a tasty new dish for lunch, or a new knitting pattern.

Imagination also helps people to create their own amusements.

4.   *Imaginative play helps children to come to terms with themselves* – Imagination provides a safety valve against many of the stresses and strains of life. A lonely child often invents an 'imaginary companion'. A child who feels helpless or oppressed in a world of strong and clever people can turn the tables in his imagination and 'pretend' to be the authority figure, i.e. Daddy, the school-master or the policeman.

Can imagination be taught?
The answer to this question is 'not really'. However, this does not mean that we can do nothing about it. It is all too easy to discourage or stunt imagination.

Parents are busy people and have not always time to wait for the child who was sent to wash his hands and is still in the bathroom pretending his fingers are high divers!

Just as imagination can easily be stunted, so too it can be encouraged.

This section suggests ways of doing this.

Imaginative Play and the handicapped child
1.   *It's not silly to pretend* – At one time many handicapped children had little opportunity to develop imaginative or make-believe play.

In fact some people thought it best *not* to encourage such pretence play in case it made their already handicapped child look 'silly' or 'different'. You may even hear such advice given today. You may be advised to concentrate only on toys and playthings which have practical educational value and which are helping your child to develop manual dexterity or other specific skills which he will need to use later on.

It certainly is important to help your child practically in this way and the other booklets in this volume suggest ways of doing this.

However, a handicapped child is a child first and handicapped second. If we deprive him of imaginative play, we are depriving him of his childhood heritage.

This kind of play is essential to the rest of his learning. He needs to be able to picture things and to use his imagination if he is to learn to communicate with others and to think for himself.

2. *Be alert to the first signs of imaginative play* – It is quite difficult to spot the first signs of imaginative play especially with a handicapped child.

His imaginative actions may be very fleeting – momentarily putting a toy cup to his mouth to 'drink' or a brief hug of a teddy bear before throwing it down.

A handicapped child, especially one who is physically handicapped, may also have insufficient hand control to show you what he is intending to do. He can become very frustrated when he *wants* to cover the doll up in bed or push the car along the road but is not able to do it. The toys won't do what he wants them to do!

3. *Join in his imaginative play* – It is important to be on the look-out for these early beginnings. Immediately you notice your child trying to hug a doll or feed it, quickly copy his actions. He will then have a good model to help him. A better understanding develops between parent and child when we appreciate what he is trying to do.

Toys and Imaginative Play
Some modern toys are so hard, detailed and shiny that they leave very little to the imagination. Simpler, home-made toys encourage the imagination far more.

A mechanical bus only lends itself to one activity, but a

wooden toy with wheels can serve many purposes – as a bus, a pram, a lorry, a car.

An Action-Man suggests mainly war-like activities, but a simpler rag figure can stand for anything – a prince or a pauper, a baby or an old man.

At first a child may need a fairly realistic toy, but later he can *pretend* with almost anything. When he has learnt to put the dolly to bed in a toy cot, he will have enough imagination to use other things, like a cardboard box as a pretend bed.

An imaginative child is always discovering new things *he* can do with his toys rather than repeating a set routine. Choose toys which lend themselves to a variety of uses.

Do not worry if your child is not using the toy the 'right' way – let him find new ways of using it himself.

Encouraging Imaginative Play

The rest of this section gives you details of ways in which you can help to encourage your child's imagination. The nature of the game will depend upon your child's stage of development. It is important to choose games and activities at the right level for your child. Not too difficult, because you will be disappointed at his lack of response and this may be stressful for him. Not too easy, as he may not respond out of boredom. To help you select suitable activities, we have prepared developmental charts.

Developmental Charts

You should find the charts useful in three ways:

1. *The charts show the stages children go through in imaginative play* – The items have been arranged in the order children usually develop them, the earliest activity is given first and the most advanced last. Thus, as you read down the charts, you will see the stages in the development of children's imaginative play.

2. *The charts give you a framework for observing your child* – The charts highlight specific activities which show the development of imaginative play. Hand him a book or a few toys, perhaps one at a time and see what he does with them.

This will give you a good idea of his stage of development in imaginative play.

Imaginative Play Charts

(i) Make-believe play

Treats all toys alike, banging or mouthing or feeling them	YES	NO	
Imitates beating on table with hand	YES	NO	*Booklet 1: Part 1*
Waves bye-bye or plays pat-a-cake in imitation	YES	NO	*Dawning Imagination*
Pushes a small car along	YES	NO	*p. 186*
Pretends to feed self, to be asleep etc.	YES	NO	
Imitates a single action in housework, e.g. brushing or dusting etc.	YES	NO	*Booklet 1: Part 2*
Engages in make-believe play – putting doll to bed, using box as car etc.	YES	NO	*Pretend Play p. 187*
Engages in prolonged domestic make-believe play involving several 'events' – e.g. feeds doll then washes it and puts it to bed etc.	YES	NO	
Engages in a lot of make-believe play, perhaps with invented people	YES	NO	*Booklet 1: Part 3*
Dresses up and pretends to be post-man, nurse etc. with appropriate actions	YES	NO	*Role Playing p. 192*

(ii) Picture Books and Stories

Recognises a few pictures of objects	YES	NO	
Listens to a short story about a picture	YES	NO	*Booklet 2: Part 1*
Recognises familiar adults in photographs	YES	NO	*Looking at Pictures p. 197*
Identifies at least seven pictures of common objects	YES	NO	

Uses actions with pictures – pretends to feed picture of doll, etc.	YES	NO
Recognises tiny details in pictures	YES	NO
Listens eagerly to stories read from picture books and likes to have them told over again	YES	NO

Booklet 2:
Part 2
Story Time
p. 203

3.   *The charts provide a means of recording your child's progress* – Beside each item you can record whether your child can (tick YES) or cannot (tick NO) do that item. If you go through the charts at regular intervals, say every six months (marking the items with different coloured pens on each occasion), you will be able to record his progress in imaginative play. This will be a great source of encouragement to you.

We suggest that you now read through the charts. Then over the next few days observe your child and record whether he can or cannot do the items as listed. Once you have done this, we can then guide you to suitable games and activities for your child.

Choosing play activities
We have grouped the imaginative play games and activities in two booklets which are further sub-divided into parts.

Booklet 1: *Let's pretend*

> Part 1: *Dawning Imagination* – very early activities
>
> Part 2: *Pretend Play* – games and make-believe
>
> Part 3: *Role Playing* – pretending to be another person.

Booklet 2: *Tell me a story*

> Part 1: *Looking at Pictures* – games involving pictures
>
> Part 2: *Story Time* – nursery rhymes and stories.

These charts will be a rough guide to help you to pick suitable activities, as parts of the booklets are indicated on the charts. For example, if your child is still banging and shaking all his toys, you will probably find Part 1 of Booklet 1 most useful, but if he is playing pretence games with his cars, try Part 2, and if he likes dressing up etc., try Part 3.

Booklet 2 is concerned with looking at pictures and story telling. Part 1 will be most useful for the child who is only beginning to recognise pictures. When he is able to listen to a short story, go onto Part 2. However, the important thing is to follow your child's lead. Note what he does, especially when he feels you're not watching him. This is the best guide of all to the games and activities your child likes best.

BOOKLET 1: LET'S PRETEND

General Hints

1. *Follow your child's lead* – You have to get 'tuned in' to your child's play so that you can join in with his pretence games.

Remember it is *his* imagination and thought which is important and you are only the helper. When you have joined in the spirit of *his* game you can then introduce new ideas gradually.

2. *Be imaginative yourself* – Some children do not play very much and hardly pretend at all. We cannot *force* them to pretend or *tell* them to do so. The best way of encouraging pretence play is to get down on the floor and start playing yourself. If your child ignores you, do not worry. Keep up the game; show him how to make teddy jump, or a puppet dance, or put a doll to bed, for a few minutes each day. Make it fun and don't be afraid to let your hair down! Your child will probably copy you in his own good time and later add his own ideas.

3. *Setting the scene* – Take the trouble to set the scene for your child while he is out of the room, or in bed, so that instead of finding his toys jumbled up in a box, he finds his dolls and teddy bears sitting around a table with food on their plates or he finds roads drawn out with his cars arranged along them.

In this way you will trigger off new ideas and keep your child's imagination alive and set him wondering what he is going to find next.

4. *Talk about it* – Imaginative games are an ideal setting for improving your child's language. Do not talk *too* much, but

match his actions with appropriate words. Say 'frog jumps' as he makes it jump and so on.

Part 1: Dawning Imagination

If your child is not yet playing imaginatively it is not too early to start to show him how. The beginning of imagination is through imitation.

If your child does not imitate your actions immediately, do not try to make him. Imitation is often deferred and you may find him suddenly copying an action you showed him a week ago.

So although you may think your actions are having no effect, keep on doing them. Your child may well be learning something from them even though he does not show it straight away.

Eat it up – The first pretence games are not played with dolls or soft toys, but are connected with the child himself. One of the earliest imaginative actions your child may do is to *pretend* to eat or *pretend* to drink from a toy cup.

The best way to encourage him to do this is to pick up pretence food and feed yourself first with great licking of lips and then give *him* some. Similarly, pretend to drink from the cup yourself and then hand it to him.

Another early pretence game is combing your hair. At first have a real comb and let your child have a go at combing your hair or his own. Then substitute the *real* comb with a cardboard *pretence* comb and do the same with this.

Soft Toys – Before handing your child a soft toy, a bear or a panda etc. have a little pretence game with the toy in front of the child. Pretend to make the toy jump off your hand for instance. You may have to do this one action many, many times before your child will start to pretend. Do not introduce more than one or two actions at first. Here are some suggestions:

(a)   Kissing the toy

(b) Cradling the toy in your arms
(c) Feeding the toy
(d) Making the toy dance
(e) Making the toy jump.

When your child starts to play with his toys in this way, gradually add more actions, but keep them very simple at this stage.

Toys on Wheels – Take a toy car or toy engine and show your child how to make it run. Add car noises and make it enjoyable. Hand him the car. If he does not get the idea, hold his hand and help him to push the car along. When he starts to get the idea, you could use two cars. You show him with one and let him copy you with the other.

Playing Bears – Rough and tumble 'pretend' games are good for getting the imagination going. Get on all fours and 'pretend' to growl like a bear or bark like a dog. Pretend to be a horse and give rides. This is a good game for Dads.

Finger Games – Finger games can have an imaginative or pretence element. Early finger games should be very simple. For instance, make your fingers walk, march or run along the table towards your child, saying 'Here comes the doggy running to you!' End up with a little tickle.

Or put caps of paper on each finger and draw a face on each. Make these finger people hide behind the toys and pop up unexpectedly. You'll be able to think up your own crazy ideas!

Part 2: Pretend Play

Mothers and Fathers – A child is indeed fortunate who is given the opportunity to watch his parents at work and given miniature tools so that he can prepare himself in pretence for activities which he will later be able to do in earnest.

At an early age a child wants a finger in every pie. Let him watch while you brush or 'hoover' the room and give him a toy brush or hoover so that he can help.

Similarly, give him his own doll's cups to 'wash up'. Let him wash his doll's clothes, and make tarts – with dough and a miniature roller.

These pretend games should not all be centred on mother's work – children should be able to watch their fathers working as well, perhaps painting, or cleaning the car or mowing the lawn. They should be given small tools or replicas so that they can pretend to help. Or even when Dad is sitting reading a newspaper and smoking a pipe, give him a piece of folded newspaper, a toy pipe to pretend with and a tin lid for an ashtray!

Doll Play – Playing with dolls or puppets is a very old kind of play. In this kind of play a child acts out his own experiences like going to bed, having a bath or going to the park. Such play is important for little boys as well as little girls. Dolls or puppets can be of either sex if dressed in slacks and can just as well be playing football as having a tea-party.

Flexible rag dolls or puppets leave more to the imagination than do very realistic dolls and action-men.

These can be home-made quite easily from plastic foam covered in stockinet. Once your child is able to carry out simple imaginative play with dolls, such as dancing the doll, or feeding the doll, he is ready for more elaborate play.

Try to have a family of dolls each with its own name – Daddy, Mummy, Bob etc. Play with your child for a few minutes each day with these toys. Set the scene, i.e., bed-time, or breakfast-time. Ideally your child needs one doll while you demonstrate with another. You can sit your doll at the table and pretend he is eating and your child can do the same with his doll. When your child can do this you can introduce another activity. Try to introduce activities which reflect your child's own experiences. If he has been away on holiday – make a little cardboard case for the dolls to put their clothes in. If you have been to the seaside, give the dolls little buckets and spades.

Helping Language – You can use your doll family to help your child's language. For example, as he makes the doll 'dance', you can say 'doll dance'. Letting each character 'dance' in turn: 'Mummy dance', 'Baby dance' etc. will help him to grasp the meaning of simple sentences.

He will then also understand these sentences when they are applied to himself. (More details for helping a child's language in doll play are given in our book *Let Me Speak*.)

Self-help Skills – Doll play is a preparation also for self-help skills – a doll can be made to do nearly all the things a child does. He can make his bed, wash his face, dress and undress, do up and undo buttons. Also you can make a book of pic-

small ball
or felt head

wool

felt glove

cardboard
roll

Sock
puppet

Felt finger puppets

Glove puppets made out of felt

Fig. 32

tures of these dolls as we will discuss in Booklet 2.

Puppets – Glove puppets can be made very simply from an old sock, felt or papier mâché or with cardboard boxes and cardboard rolls, see Fig. 32.

Show your child how the puppet can 'wave bye-bye' or 'eat his dinner' or 'clap his hands'. You can use the puppet in the doll play or when telling simple stories or rhymes, e.g. the puppet can 'eat the bread and honey' when the king is in the counting house!

Later your child himself will be able to bring the puppet to life and make him do simple actions.

Shy children often speak more with a puppet in their hands.

Junk – Infant teachers are great collectors of junk; cotton reels, empty egg boxes, cardboard rolls, match-boxes and yoghurt cartons. They know that these are often more 'educational' than many of the toys bought in shops, because they feed the children's imagination (see section on *Exploratory Play*, p. 44).

Here are some uses of junk:

1. *Model making* – With a little imagination, paper and glue, models can be made from junk material. At first the models

cardboard snout   cardboard tail

Egg-box dragon

Cotton reel snake

Fig. 33

will have to be very simple and you will have to help to make them. Cotton reels can have simple faces painted on them and become 'men'. With paper hats they can be policemen, sailors, soldiers, firemen etc. Seeing them come to life will help your child's imagination. Fig. 33 shows a fearsome dragon which can be made out of egg boxes, or a snake out of cotton reels. As we said before, some of the best toys for your child are free.

2. *Houses* – It is very easy to make simple houses out of stiff paper as you can see from Fig. 34. At first you will have to

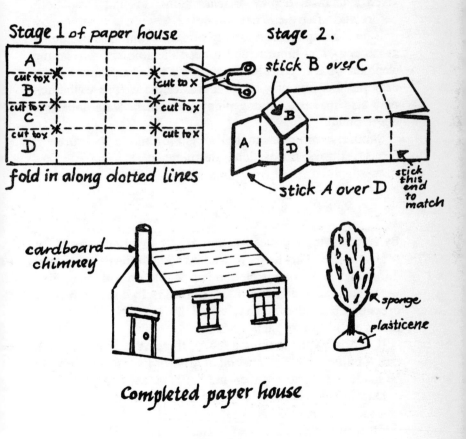

Fig. 34

make them for your child, but let him watch you and do as much as he can and help with the painting.

Much imaginative play can centre around a pretence village, especially if you put your houses on a large sheet of card and draw roads, gardens etc. around them. You can add trees made out of sponge and a plasticene base and pillar boxes made out of cotton reels painted red. Match-box cars can also be used as well as models of people and animals.

3. *Special Outings and Occasions* – A child will benefit a great deal more from special outings and occasions if he is given a chance to play *pretence* games around them both before and after the event.

If he is going to the zoo, buy him some animals, use boxes as cages and let him pretend to feed the animals; ride on the elephant's back etc. If he does not get the idea, show him by example. Let him play with these after the visit as well. Such play also makes a talking point and will help his language development.

Similarly, models can be bought or made to represent farms, railways, fire-stations, shops etc.

Part 3: Role Playing

By role playing we mean acting a part or pretending to be someone else. This helps your child to act out his emotional difficulties and to appreciate other people's positions in life.

Dressing-up clothes – It is important to have a box of dressing-up clothes handy, especially hats. Nothing transforms a child more than a head-dress.

It is worthwhile making a few of these. A crown, a nurse's hat, a pirate's hat and an Indian head-dress, can very simply be made out of card, paper and feathers, see Fig. 35.

Dad's shirt will make a long coat for a child. A few pairs of shoes are also appreciated.

Theatrical shops sell beards etc. or they can be made out of wool, fur fabric etc.

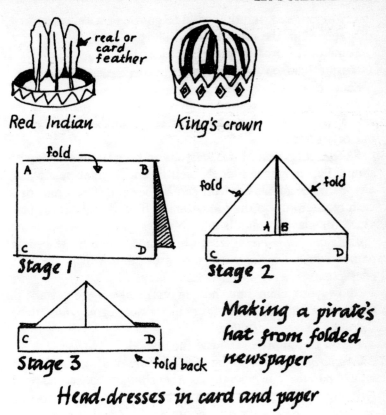

real or card feather

Red Indian

King's crown

fold

A   B

C   D

Stage 1

fold   fold

A B

C   D

Stage 2

C   D

Stage 3 ← fold back

Making a pirate's hat from folded newspaper

Head-dresses in card and paper

Fig. 35

A handicapped child may be very good at this kind of play and may be able to impersonate characters very amusingly. However, some children have few ideas to start with and you will have to get them going. Show them how the queen sits on her throne and the people bow to her, and so on.

Pretend Games – Children should be encouraged to play pretend games together. This helps them to get on with other people.

A handicapped child often finds this very difficult and other children may not want to play with him if he 'spoils the game'.

Try to persuade another child to go round with him at first and 'show him the ropes'.

Some of the most popular games are:

Hospital game   Cops and robbers
Schools   Keeping shop

Props – It will encourage role playing if you provide a few simple props. A Wendy house or shop can be simply made out of a screen.

Keep a collection of tins, cartons and egg boxes for playing shops. Papier mâché models of fruit and vegetables etc. can also be made or plastic fruit can be bought. Toy scales or a cash register add to the fun. A small blackboard can be provided for playing schools and so on.

Let's be giants etc. – There are some active make-believe games which do not need any props but which are very energetic.

Show your child how he can jump like a frog, walk in strides like a giant, on all fours like a bear or wiggling along the floor like a caterpillar.

If you can improvise music for this, all the better.

Drama and Mime – In the simplest form of drama and mime which parents can encourage, the child is concerned with re-living a simple event which he has seen or heard about.

Here are some ways of encouraging this activity:

What am I doing? – In this game you mime an action, like hammering, eating or driving a car and your child guesses what you are doing. If he cannot tell you what you are doing at first, he can copy your actions. Then encourage him to do the actions first for you to guess. Make a fuss of him when he invents new actions.

Who am I? – The idea is to mime the activity of someone at work, e.g. a fisherman baiting his hook, casting his line, getting a bite, reeling it in and getting the fish off the hook and dropping it into his net.

If two or more people are involved, then one person can do the miming and the others can guess who he is pretending to be.

This gives you an opportunity to help your child to elaborate his mime by giving him a model.

At first, the mime will have to be very simple and concerned with some person or event which is very familiar.

Here are a few suggestions: the dustman, the lollipop man, a traffic policeman, a man mending the road, a gardener, a window cleaner, bus conductor etc.

Action stories – Some of the best stories are ones you make up using your child as the main character. These stories can simply recount the events of the day or a special occasion (going on holiday; visit to the zoo). Or they can be totally imaginary, e.g. 'John and the fearful dragon'. As you tell the story you could also encourage your child to act out the different actions. The more varied these are, the better.

The actions in nursery rhymes and stories can also be mimed. If you recite the rhyme or tell the story, your child can put in the actions.

This can begin with simple action rhymes and songs like: 'Round and round the village' or 'This is the way we wash our clothes'. Later you can develop freer or more creative actions to other rhymes and stories, e.g. The Little Red Hen; The Gingerbread Man.

Putting on a play – The next step is to act a story with more than one person taking part. This helps children to co-operate with others. Perhaps other children in the family, or a few friends, could take part.

It is best to concentrate on actions at first, rather than words, and for the parents to provide the words of the story. Certainly you do not want to make your child 'learn a part'. However, you may find that he naturally begins to join in with the words in 'The Gingerbread Man' and that's fine.

Let the children dress up and perform their play within the family circle and get clapped and so on. No attempt should be made to *train* a finished performance – this would have the effect of damping down the child's imagination instead of fostering it.

A Puppet Play – Instead of acting themselves, some children find it less inhibiting to use puppets as the actors. A stage for a puppet play can easily be constructed (see Fig. 36) or an improvised stage made from chairs.

It is a good thing to suggest a theme or character for your child.

The puppet could be a dancer, an acrobat, a footballer etc. Perhaps he will like to base puppets on some of the television characters, i.e. Lamb Chop or Sooty.

Two children together of course can act little scenes; a boxing match, Punch and Judy, or some of the fables with two characters.

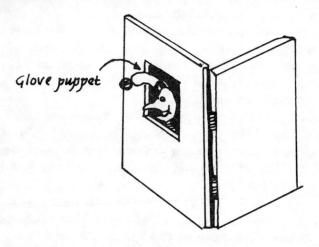

Glove puppet

Puppet theatre from simple screen

Fig. 36

BOOKLET 2: TELL ME A STORY

Part 1: Looking at pictures

A young baby or immature child first learns to recognise his mother's face and after that a few familiar objects and toys which are important to him.

His face will light up when he sees his milk, or beads or panda. It will be some time before he starts to recognise pictures of these objects; it takes a mental effort to transform black and coloured marks on paper into a banana or a bus.

This booklet will suggest ways of encouraging your child to make mental pictures and also recognise pictures on paper.

The First Picture Book – A child's first picture books should be of very familiar objects or favourite toys. This is why it is best to make your own. You know best what your child likes and what his toys look like.

Look out for pictures in magazines or mail-order catalogues and cut them out or order some 'Early Language Stamps' from Learning Development Aids (L.D.A.) which are pictures of common objects. You can even cut out some of the pictures in cheap picture books (e.g. Ladybird Books). If there is an 'artist' in the family who can draw simple objects this is better still or you could take colour photographs of his favourite toys.

The first book need only contain three or four pictures and should be made of stout paper or thin card or cloth and preferably covered with transparent plastic (Fig. 37 shows you various ways of making this book). One of the pictures could be of your face. Alternatively, you can buy small photograph albums from stationery shops, Boots etc. and put the pictures

Zig-zag book

staples

Single pages stapled together

Home-made books

Fig. 37

in these. The main advantage of these is that you can easily change the pictures, making an entirely new book in a few minutes!

Make it a Treat – If your child enjoys his first introduction to books he will probably learn to love them. Make looking at books a special treat. Choose your time: when he is not anxious to rush off and when *you* can be relaxed and close to your child. Remember, a child cannot concentrate for a long time. Start with a few minutes a day, and gradually increase the length of time spent with a book.

Don't seem bored – A child's first picture book is not very exciting reading for Mum. However, *you* must treat it as if it were. If *you* seem bored, so will he be. Turn the pages of the book as if on a voyage of discovery.

If your child shows no interest in pictures yet, you will need to go through these stages:

Stage 1 – What is it? – For this game as well as your first book, you will need real objects ready to hand. If the pictures are of a shoe, Mummy, ball and a biscuit, have these (the shoe, ball and biscuit) ready in a box.

First point to Mummy or pull an object out of the box and name it and then turn the pages of the book until you find a picture to match.

Put the object on or beside the picture and point first to one and then the other and name them. 'Look, here's a *shoe*, and *here's a shoe.*'

When you have repeatedly shown your child the object and its picture, you can start giving him a more active role. Hold up the object, a ball, and say 'BALL' and let him turn the pages until he finds the right picture.

Alternatively, hold up a PICTURE and let *him* find the *object* which goes with it.

When your child can match objects and pictures, you can use the book on its own as follows:

Stage 2 – Where is it? – This time give your child the book and tell him – 'Find the shoe'. Praise him when he finds it and help him if necessary.

Picture Cube

Fig. 38

Picture Cubes – Pictures do not need to be only in books. An enjoyable and educational toy is a picture cube.

This can be made from milk cartons (see Fig. 38), beer mats or expanded polystyrene sheeting.

Pictures of familiar objects are stuck on each face of the cube.

Play *Where's it Gone* with the cube as well as with the book. When your child has found the right picture, let him have a little game with the cube – throwing it to you.

Picture Roundabouts – A picture roundabout is like a picture cube, but is mounted on a rod (e.g. a blunted knitting needle) so that it swivels round (see Fig. 39).

Immature, physically handicapped or non-ambulant children can often get lots of fun out of this plaything. Again, you should name the object and encourage your child to spin

Picture Roundabout

Fig. 39

the roundabout and stop it at the right place.

(Some of the books in the Barnaby Series by L.D.A. will give you some more suggestions for ways in which you can help your child to recognise objects: *First Pictures* and *Learn to Look*.)

Match Box Game – Collect some old match boxes and glue the trays so that they are sticking half-way out of the covers. Paint the boxes in different colours with quick drying enamel and paste little pictures onto the covers. (L.D.A's Phonic stamps are a good size to use.)

Have two pictures of each of your child's favourite objects. Show your child how to slide one box onto the tray of another. Then tell him which picture to choose, e.g. 'spoon', and praise him when he chooses the right one. Then say 'find another spoon', and see if he can find the second picture. This picture matching is helping him to recognise pictures.

Dominoes – Picture dominoes can also be made from match boxes, or from pieces of plywood. In this game there are two pictures on each domino and so it is a little more difficult than the match box game. However, the game is played in exactly the same way as ordinary dominoes.

Let's pretend with pictures – As soon as your child is taking an interest in pictures and turning over the pages, you can introduce a simple imaginative action. Choose one of his favourite pictures, a dog perhaps. Every time you turn up this picture, give the dog a pat, saying 'Good dog'. Your child will probably copy your action before he copies what you say. This is helping him to enjoy the book, to use his imagination and also to use language.

Introduce actions with one of the pictures only at first. When your child is using these actions, extend your imagination to another picture (pretend to bounce the ball, etc.).

After a time you can introduce actions on every page. You can 'feed teddy', 'bounce the ball', 'brush your hair', 'dance the doll', and so on. Telling your child to 'feed teddy' etc. will also be a great help to his understanding of language, which is best learnt through active participation.

What is he doing? – The first picture books will be pictures of objects, but when your child is recognising these well, you should then introduce pictures with actions in them. Tell your child what 'Peter' is doing and ask him to tell you. If your child cannot *tell* you what the people are doing, let him *mime* the actions instead. In Collins Picture Lions series there is an excellent picture book of actions called *Hop, Skip and Jump*.

Picture Posting – Prepare a posting-box by cutting a slit into the side or top of a cardboard box. Use cards with pictures of common objects pasted on them. Spread them out on the table and tell your child which one to post. If he picks the right picture, let him post it in the box and give him a clap. If he should choose the wrong one, hold your hand over the posting slit until he changes it for the correct picture.

Alternatively, hold the pictures up one at a time and get

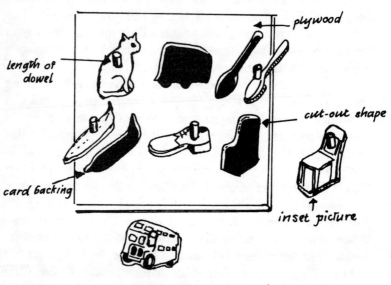

Simple Formboard

Fig. 40

him to *name* the picture and as he names a picture correctly, give it to him to post and give him a little clap.

Picture form-boards – Place five or six boldly coloured pictures of familiar objects onto a sheet of plywood. Draw the outline round each picture on the wood and cut out with a fretsaw. Sandpaper each piece and try for fit. Stick a sheet of cardboard onto the back of the plywood sheet and stick the pictures onto their cut-out shapes. Glue a short length of dowelling into the centre of each picture to make a handle (see Fig. 40).

The game is in fitting each cut-out picture into place. At first let your child play with the board and remove the pictures one at a time.

Start showing him how to replace them with one picture at a time. Show him where the picture goes and then put it on the table for him to replace. Not only do children enjoy this game, it is also an aid to picture recognition, as he is learning to identify pictures by their outline shape.

Part 2: Story Time

Picture Stories – The basic ingredients of a story are simply a character and some action. We have to go right back to these basics when telling children their first stories. Pictures also help your child to imagine what is happening.

The pictures – paste several pictures onto stiff cards (four inches square is a good size). Make sure that some of the cards are pictures of characters: teddy bear, doll, dog, bird, Mummy, baby, Daddy etc.

The other cards can be of *objects* or *places*: apple, orange, chair, cups, car, house etc.

Make sure your child can recognise these pictures before starting simple stories and then place one character card on the table and start telling the story '...Here is Daddy. What is he going to do today? First he's going to eat ... (At this point pick up a picture of an apple) ... an APPLE'.

The first story need be no longer than this, or as well as eating an apple, Daddy might eat a banana, some toast etc.

Do not feel you have to think out a new story every time. All children enjoy the repetition of stories and at this stage it is doubly important. As your child becomes familiar with the story, let him choose the pictures and tell the story.

Sequence Stories in Pictures – First stories are concerned with one character and one action. Later a child learns to understand sequences of actions. For instance, a child gets up, eats breakfast, puts on his coat, goes out of the door, rides his tricycle etc. For this game, a separate card is prepared with a picture of each action. At first you will have to pick up each card in order, as you tell the story, but in time he will be able to arrange the pictures in order himself and tell his own story. Several sets of sequence story cards should be prepared. Once he has got hold of the idea, give your child a new set of cards which he has not seen before and let him tell his own story with these. (Galt's and L.D.A. sell sets of sequence pictures.)

A magnet board or flannel board can also be used for sequence stories.

Drawing Stories – If you can draw a little, this is a great asset when you are introducing stories.

Use a blackboard and chalk or some cheap paper (e.g. lining paper obtainable in wall paper shops) and crayons. Draw simple stick figures and animals and houses etc., as you go along with the narrative. This helps your child's attention and sense of anticipation. He becomes an active participant in the story.

A Child's own Story Book – As soon as your child is able to draw a circle, or even before, you can start scrap-books of his own drawings. It is better to have a number of short books (just one or two pages) rather than one long book. Get him to tell you about his pictures. Write what he tells you under each picture. At first he may simply name each object, i.e. 'that's a ball'. You can add a few more ideas. ('It's Peter's football. He's kicked a goal.')

As your child grows older his books will become longer and

more detailed and you could write or type the story at the bottom of each page.

Scrap-Book Stories – Collect all kinds of pictures cut out from magazines, catalogues, Christmas cards and books. Keep these together in a box. Get your child to help you to choose four or five pictures and to arrange them nicely on a page and stick them on.

Make up a story around these pictures, and write or type it out and stick it on the page.

Made-up Stories – Some of the best stories are those made up on the spur of the moment by parents for their children.

These can be tailor-made for the individual child and he can even feature as the main character. The most successful stories will be told over and over again. Their familiarity gives him confidence but, through them also, his horizons can be widened. The child can be an active participant in such stories and take his turn to add an incident.

Nursery Rhymes and Singing Games – Children are often introduced to nursery rhymes which are far beyond their comprehension.

When they 'recite' these rhymes it is obvious that the words mean nothing to them, but are a jumble of sounds which go up and down in interesting ways. Nevertheless, children will enjoy the rhythm for its own sake.

Children are less at sea if the first rhymes are short and, more important, incorporate activities.

Here are some suggestions: 'Ring-a-ring-of-roses', 'Round and round the garden', 'Here we go round the Mulberry bush', 'Hickory-Dickory-Dock', 'Incy-Wincy spider', 'I'm a little teapot, short and stout', 'Baa-baa-black-sheep'.

Later the longer nursery rhymes can form the basis of mime and play acting and puppetry.

(Ladybird produce inexpensive collections of nursery rhymes. A good selection is *Mother Goose Treasury*, Puffin Picture Books.)

Folk Tales – The first folk tales to tell should contain plenty of repetition. Some suggestions are: The Gingerbread Boy, The

Story of the Three Little Pigs, The Story of the Three Bears, The Little Red Hen, The Turnip and the Three Billy-Goats-Gruff. (Ladybird Books, *The Fairy Tale Treasury* – Puffin Books.)

It is important to find the time to read or tell these stories to your child over and over again so that he begins to join in and pick out his favourite story. Encourage him to act the stories or mime them and use them as the basis of a puppet play.

Longer stories like The Golden Goose, Rumpelstiltskin, Cinderella, Little Red Riding Hood, Puss-in-Boots, The Elves and the Shoemaker can also be found in *The Fairy Tale Treasury*. Gradually introduce these longer stories when you feel your child is ready.

SECTION 6: PUZZLE-IT-OUT PLAY

Introduction
Booklet 1: How does it work?
Booklet 2: Like and unlike

INTRODUCTION TO PUZZLE-IT-OUT PLAY

This section is all about problem-solving and puzzling things out. A child is, of course, solving problems in many of the games we have already described in other sections. In our section on *Skilful Play*, for example, the child is constantly working things out as he acquires new hand skills. But while the main concern in that section was with acquiring hand skills, the purpose of this section is to develop the child's ability to puzzle things out. In addition, the emphasis in this section is not on solving problems concerning the child's own actions but rather on solving problems related to the world around him.

We face such problems every day – How can I avoid that traffic jam on the way to work? Why don't my roses grow so well in this part of the garden? How will I get that stain out of the carpet?

Whether or not we solve such problems depends, in part, on what we know about the problem (for example, what other roads lead round the traffic jam, or what sorts of soils are best for growing roses), but it also depends on how we use this knowledge. It depends, in fact, on the way we think.

Thinking is a skill, just like drawing a picture or riding a bicycle. Like all skills, it develops through use. Young children develop their thinking skills through trying to satisfy their curiosity about the world around them. Things which seem commonplace to us are often a source of wonder for a child. Why is it that when Mummy pushes that thing on the wall the light goes on in the middle of the room? Why can't I roll bricks along the floor? Why does the room go cloudy when the kettle whistles? How can I get the sweet out of that bottle?

And quite often, when we see our child seemingly just 'messing about' with his toys or other objects, he isn't just keeping his hands busy. Likely as not he is trying to understand something. We call this Puzzle-it-out Play.

The Importance of Puzzle-it-out Play

1.　*Puzzle-it-out Play develops the child's thinking skills* – The child who attempts to solve a puzzle or a problem is not passively taking in information about the task in hand. Rather, he is actively using his knowledge and his powers of thinking in order to work out the solution. Such solutions very often demand the ability to detect which are the significant features of the problem and which factors can be ignored. The youngster who is learning to sort different objects into piles of red ones and blue ones is also learning that he has to ignore their irrelevant characteristics, like shape, feel, smell, size, weight etc. This is a skill which all children have to learn. They learn this skill by practice in solving puzzles and problems. In short, Puzzle-it-out Play helps the child to learn how to think.

2.　*Puzzle-it-out Play encourages the child's curiosity* – The child who successfully solves a problem is thereby rewarded for his curiosity. His success will encourage him to be curious about fresh puzzles in the future. This is vitally important for, as we have said before, curiosity is the driving force behind much of the child's learning. Puzzle-it-out Play, therefore, encourages the child to learn more about the world about him.

3.　*Puzzle-it-out Play encourages independence* – The child who solves (or even attempts to solve) a puzzle is, in effect, thinking for himself. However much we may help him, his final solutions and thus his new discoveries are really his very own. Puzzle-it-out Play thus encourages the child's confidence in his ability to solve his own problems.

Puzzle-it-out Play and the Handicapped Child

We have stressed the importance of curiosity and the ability to puzzle things out in the development of all children. It is often said, though, that handicapped children are noticeably lacking in this interest in the world around them. In contrast with the seemingly unending curiosity of most young children, some handicapped children often seem to be very passive and unconcerned about things around them. Yet again, other handicapped children appear very distractable – seemingly unable to concentrate on anything for more than a few moments.

How, then, can you help your child to develop such curiosity, to want to puzzle things out?

First of all, you can 'whet his appetite' by showing him that his world is full of interesting objects and events – things he can be curious about. This, of course, is the main theme of our section on *Exploratory Play*. You should, we suggest, use *Exploratory Play* and this section together.

Second, you should pay close attention to those things which your child is most curious about. Like all of us, he won't be interested in everything but he will be interested in something. It is through his current interests that you will help build his capacity for puzzling things out. This point is absolutely vital. As the saying goes – you can lead a horse to water but you can't make him drink. Even the best thought-out games will fall flat if your child is not interested in playing them.

Third, you can encourage your child's desire to puzzle things out by presenting him with puzzles which he *can* solve. We would all very quickly get fed up with any problem which we had no chance of solving. Therefore it is very important to present your child with puzzles at the appropriate level of difficulty. You will thus be giving him the chance to experience the satisfaction of having solved a challenging problem.

Fourth, and this point really follows from the last one, you should give your child the *opportunity* to solve puzzles and problems. This means that you have to resist the natural inclination to help your child every time he gets into the slightest difficulties over a problem. Rather, you must let him puzzle out his own solution. This may take some time, of course, but he will, in fact, learn more through his errors than his successes. If you step in too quickly to help him, then you are, in effect, doing his thinking for him. This is not really helping him. The most important help that you can give is to present him with problems at the correct level of difficulty for him: problems which present a challenge but which he can solve.

In most of the games in this section we show you how you can start with a relatively simple game and gradually make it more difficult. But, as a rule of thumb, think how many *new* skills are required in order to play the game. If your child has to learn more than one or two, then this game is probably too difficult for him. So try a simpler version of the game or change to another game.

Encouraging Puzzle-it-out Play

In the remaining part of this section we have put forward some games which you can play with your child to encourage his Puzzle-it-out Play.

As we have pointed out, the key to encouraging your child's powers of thinking is to give him problems which are sufficiently difficult to interest him but not so difficult as to daunt his curiosity. Even for any one child, this correct level of difficulty can vary a lot, depending on the type of problem posed. This is quite natural when you think about it. The skilled cabinet-maker, who can solve very tricky woodworking problems, may be totally foxed by the simplest of, say, gardening problems.

For this reason we have not provided development charts to guide you in your choice of the appropriate game to play with your child. But what we have done is to indicate, for each game, the kinds of skills which are necessary for this game to be appropriate for your child. If your child does not have these skills then we refer you to games in other chapters which will help him gain such skills.

Booklet 1, *How Does it Work?*, is a collection of games which really reflect the title. Your child has to solve the problem by discovering how things work.

Booklet 2, *Like and Unlike*, consists of games which encourage your child to think of the similarities and differences among a range of objects. This kind of thinking is important to the development of concepts. Concepts do not refer to individual objects but rather to groups or classes of objects. 'Men', 'animals', 'flowers', 'furniture' are words reflecting concepts. Concepts can also refer to common properties of different objects – like colour, or shape, or weight. When you consider it, much of our thinking is through the use of concepts.

We suggest that you look briefly through both booklets so that you can get the 'flavour' of the games. Then choose or adapt those which are the most suitable for your child.

Above all, we would like to finish with a point which we have already made in this and in previous chapters. You will be most successful if you tailor your games to fit in with your child's current interests and activities. This is particularly relevant in games which depend almost entirely on your child's curiosity.

BOOKLET 1: HOW DOES IT WORK?

The object of the games in this booklet is to pose an interesting problem or puzzle for your child. In order to solve the puzzle your child must have certain skills. These skills are noted at the beginning of each game. You will find that all these skills can be developed through playing games which we have suggested in some of the previous sections, especially *Exploratory Play* and *Skilful Play*. If your child does not yet have these skills, then we refer you to relevant games and activities in the other sections which will help him to acquire such skills.

Looked at in another way, of course, the games in this booklet follow on naturally from the games in previous sections. They provide your child with a fresh interest in the skills he has learned and they give him further opportunities for using these skills.

The games in this booklet should be considered as examples of how you can turn Exploratory Play or Skilful Play into Puzzle-it-out Play. We hope that they will spark off your own ideas for your own games. You are in the best position to decide on games for your child because you can find out most about his present interests. As we have said before, this is the key to Puzzle-it-out Play.

Stack-Packs – For this game, your child should be able to build a fairly straight tower of at least six small bricks (see *Skilful Play*, p. 128).

For this game you will need a set of four small nesting tables. Nesting boxes will do (many toyshops sell them) but tables are better because you can see how they fit on top of each other as in Fig. 41. If you cannot buy these tables you will find them easy to make out of hard-board or perspex. The interesting feature of these nesting tables is that they make quite different stacks depending on the order in which they are piled on each other. If you start with the smallest and add the next biggest table one by one, you will obtain a nest of tables. On the other hand, if you start with the

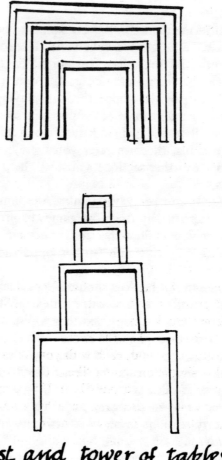

Nest and tower of tables

Fig. 41

biggest and then take each smaller one in turn you will build a tower.

At first, give your child only two of the tables, say the largest and the smallest. Let him explore them thoroughly. If he does not stack them, then you should model the stacks for him. Once he is familiar with the two tables, give him the third (just two tables will be pretty boring after a while) and then, later on, the fourth. Allow him to experiment with different combinations of the tables.

To be able to make either of the stacks shown, requires the understanding that objects can be arranged in an ordered series, according to their size. This is actually quite a difficult idea for young children to grasp, so at first do not expect your child to produce either of the stacks given in Fig. 41. It is more likely that he will make a stack like the ones in Fig. 42. Do not worry if your child makes stacks like these for this is a natural stage in any child's development. It is only through trying different combinations of the tables that your child will learn that they can be ordered in a series. So resist the temptation to prompt him into 'acting correctly'. Certainly you can show him that a 'nest' or a 'tower' can be made, but *don't* force him to imitate you. In this game he will learn more through his own errors rather than by being restricted to the 'correct' stacking sequences.

Build one like mine – For this game your child should be capable of grasping and stacking bricks (see *Skilful Play*, p. 128). Your child can apply these skills to copying the structures that you build with bricks.

Sit opposite your child, each with your own pile of bricks. Now build a simple structure, like a tower of three bricks, and see if your child builds one like it. If he doesn't copy you, this does not matter. He may have his own plans for his bricks. But your job is to show him what can be done with the bricks. You are providing him with models to copy if he wants to.

Of course, it may be that a tower of three bricks is rather boring, so introduce some variety – but keep them simple. In

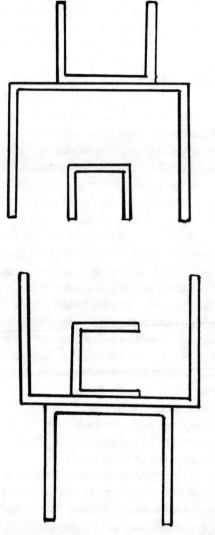

Intermediate table stacks

Fig. 42

Fig. 43 we show two very simple models for your child to copy – a pyramid and a bridge. We think they are simple but, of course, they are harder than building a straight tower, where the bricks simply go on top of each other. The bridge, for example, demands that the two bottom bricks be only a certain distance apart and that the top brick is placed exactly in between them.

You will have noticed that both these structures can be extended to use many more than three bricks. You can make a larger pyramid or a long rampart wall. And let's not forget that they can be built in three dimensions as well. If you have oblong bricks (you can easily make them by glueing two or three bricks together), you can introduce more ambitious designs.

Obviously, you have a lot of scope here. What is more, these games lead onto more advanced constructional games like Lego.

But remember to proceed stage by stage. Only give your child models that he can understand and copy. As he gets more adept at working out the structures then keep his interest up with more complex designs.

Pick-a-String – For this game your child should be capable of grasping small objects between finger and thumb (see *Skilful Play*, p. 116).

The object of the game is to pull in an attractive toy which is fastened to a length of string, about 1 ft long. Set the toy in front of your child, but far enough away so that he has to use the string to retrieve it.

Does he find this easy? Good – now let's make it a bit harder. Lay out two or three extra strings, parallel to the one with the toy. Now he has to choose which string will get him the toy. He shouldn't have too much difficulty working this one out – but if he does, then give him extra practice using only one 'spare' string at first. Alternatively, use strings of different colours.

You've realised by now that this game can get harder and harder. When your child can choose correctly between four

Building with bricks
Build one like this

A pyramid

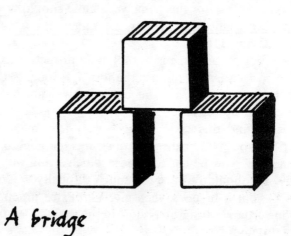

A bridge

Fig. 43

parallel strings, you can then set the strings out in a criss-cross pattern, as in Fig. 44. This is much more difficult

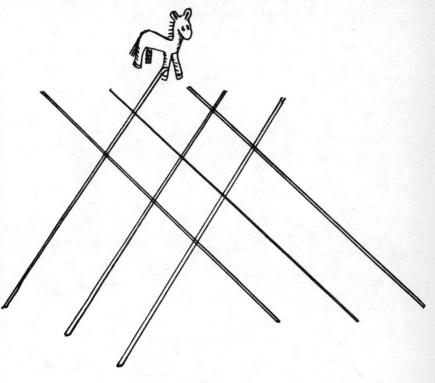

Criss-cross pick-a-string

Fig. 44

because although the toy is right in front of him, the correct string to pull is away to his left. Give him plenty of practice at this stage, varying the position of the toy and the direction of the string, sometimes to the left, sometimes to the right. Remember, the spirit of the game is all-important here. He's trying to get the toy and you're trying to fox him. Don't make it too difficult but keep up the friendly challenge. And when he gets the toy, make a big fuss of him.

As he gets more adept at this game you could add more strings, or place them closer together. You need not restrict yourself to a criss-cross pattern, of course, but you can use curly arrangements, as in Fig. 45. These can be very difficult so use only two or three strings at first.

Curly pick-a-string

Fig. 45

As variations of this game you could cover the strings with a napkin so that only the ends are showing. Now your child has to visualise the path of the correct string until it reappears on his side of the napkin. This game is only possible with straight-line patterns, of course, so you should start with parallel strings and then introduce the criss-cross patterns.

If your child becomes really expert at the game but still enjoys playing it, you could blind-fold him so that he can only choose the correct string by feeling the weight of the toy at the end of it.

Switch Threading – For this game your child should be capable of two-handed threading games (see *Skilful Play*, p. 127).

This game is a real puzzler. The object is to thread some flat circular wooden chips onto a thin string. But this string is fastened to a short dowel rod (1″ long and ½″ thick) at one end and to a small-disc (¾″ wide and ¼″ thick) at the other end, as in Fig. 46. What is more, the chips which have to be threaded have two kinds of holes – a circle and a slot (see Fig. 46). The handyman in the family can easily make all these pieces. The important thing is the various sizes involved. The dowel rod should be slightly longer and thicker than the slots in the chips and the disc should be slightly bigger than the circular hole in the chips.

This is the secret of the whole game for it would be natural to think that the rod goes into the slots and the disc goes into the circular holes. But, of course, they won't quite fit.

The solution (you've guessed it! – or have you?) is to thread the rod through the holes and to slide the disc through the slots. This solution requires a switch from the 'apparent' solution of the problem. Furthermore, it requires that the rod and the disc be threaded end-on rather than side-on (that's why we use thin string).

To show your child what the 'finished product' looks like, it will be useful to have a spare 'switch-thread' with all the chips on it. Alternatively, you can simply show him the chips

switch threader

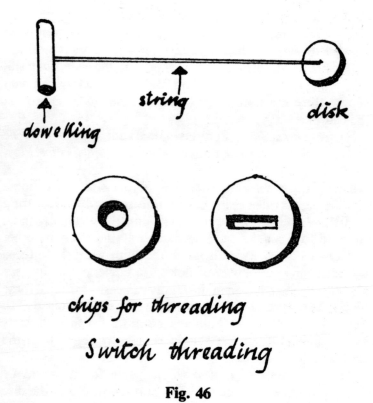

chips for threading

Switch threading

Fig. 46

on the thread and then, out of sight, unthread the chips. Now just lay out the chips in front of him and hand him the thread!

At first, give your child the chance to work out the solution by himself. If he does so, he will be thrilled (and so will you!).

However, if you find that he is not making any progress towards solving the problem, you can give him some clues:
1. Take away the 'slotted' chips, leaving the ones with circular holes. Then lay the string out in front of him and

turn the dowel rod until it points the same way as the string. See if your child can work out the rest of the solution.

2. If that doesn't work, even after some time, pick up the dowel rod (still parallel to the string) and give it to your child, making sure that he holds it the same way, i.e. like a needle and thread.

3. Finally, you can actually take his hand and help him thread the rod through the hole in one of the chips.

Hopefully, he will now have got the idea and will go on to thread the disc in the same way. But if not, you can give him similar clues to those outlined above.

But remember – this is a puzzle game and the main idea is to discover the solution. Don't give your child prompts unless you really have to. The more he finds out for himself, the greater will be his joy. So give him *plenty of time* to work things out.

However, even if you had to prompt him through every step of the solution, make a big fuss of him when he finally gets there. For his eventual discovery, even though quite small to you, will be very important to him. So make his discovery worthwhile!

Colour Mixing – When your child has begun to develop his painting skills (see *Skilful Play*, p. 132), he will no doubt be splashing different colours all over the paper and in the process, these colours will mix to form new ones. And when he is washing the brush out in the jam jar, the water will change colour with every new shade of paint. He may have noticed himself that the colours change when mixed – if not, you can draw his attention to it yourself. No doubt he will want to experiment for himself, by mixing colours on the paper and in the jam jar.

This early messing about is, in fact, very important and you should give him plenty of opportunity to play with colours in this way. However, this 'accidental' mixing does have two drawbacks. First, not all colours mix very well – they don't necessarily make distinctive new shades and thus aren't very interesting. Second, it may be very difficult for your child to remember which were the colours that made his new mixture of orange or violet.

So, after your child has had *a lot* of experience in messing about, here is a game to help your child understand how colours can be mixed to form new colours. You will need some large sheets of paper, some brushes, and poster paints in the basic colours of black, white, red, blue and yellow.

Draw two overlapping circles on a sheet of paper. Then paint each circle a separate colour, say blue and yellow. The result, as we indicate in Fig. 47, is that the two colours com-

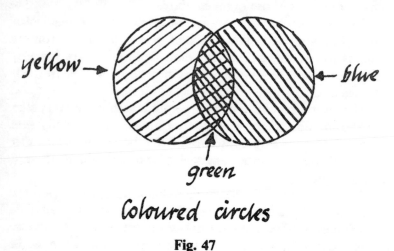

yellow → ← blue

green

Coloured circles

Fig. 47

bine to produce green where the circles overlap. The advantage of the overlapping circles is, of course, that you can see what the original colours are that make the new one.

Now let your child have a go. Have a good supply of 'circled' paper handy so that he has a lot of practise with different colour combinations. Only let him use two colours on each sheet of paper and choose, first, those which produce the most distinctive new colours (Aha! Can you remember them? If not, get in some sneak practice!).

You should insist that he only paints in the circles (use

physical prompts if necessary), otherwise this could become a random daubing game.

And when he has successfully completed a few colour combinations, why not pin the sheets up on the wall as his own colour chart?

Pour me a tune – For this game your child should be able to pour from a cup or a jug (see *Exploratory Play*, p. 45) and should be able to use a stick for banging or hammering (see *Skilful Play*, p. 121) or playing a xylophone (see *Exploratory Play*, p. 46).

This game is a continuation of the 'Musical Hammering' game which we described in *Exploratory Play*, p. 46. The basic idea is to produce different musical notes by striking jars filled with varying amounts of water. The novel element in this version is that your child makes his own notes by pouring the water himself.

As before, you will need some jam jars, a jug of water and a stick. Demonstrate the game by pouring water into one jar, tapping it with the stick so that your child can hear the notes rising with the water level. Then do the same with two or three more jars, but leave the water level different in each.

Now pour all the water back into the jug and let him have a go. At first he may need some help, so you could strike the jar while he pours, or vice versa. If there is another musical instrument (an ordinary xylophone for example) in the house, you can have a lot of fun matching the notes on the water jars.

A word of warning. It is likely that at least some water will be spilled during this game, so make sure that you play it where this will not matter.

Lucky Dip – This game develops out of the hiding games and the 'Surprise Packet' game which we described in *Exploratory Play*, p. 44.

The idea of this game is for your child to reach for a toy which is covered by a cloth. As he cannot see it he has to recognise it only by feeling it.

You will need a selection of small toys. Some of your child's favourite dangling toys (see *Exploratory Play*, p. 32), but minus the elastic, will be ideal. He will be familiar with how they look and will now be learning to match what he sees with what he feels.

Place a toy underneath an old duster, or a small tablecloth or blanket, and encourage your child to feel for it. Your child may initially want to remove the cloth, so use a board onto which you can fasten the cloth by drawing pins, nails etc. Don't use your best tablecloth, but something which you don't mind going ragged at the edges!

At first, use only one toy at a time. Then introduce two or three so that he can choose between them. If your child can understand verbal demands, you can ask him to find 'the ball' or 'the cube' or 'the doll'.

Alternatively, if you have duplicates of the toys you could simply hold one up for him to find the matching toy.

As a further variation, you could draw pictures of the toys and get him to feel for the matching toy by showing him the pictures one by one.

Note however, that these last two games involve 'matching' skills which may be beyond your child's current level of ability (we describe other 'matching games' in the next booklet, p. 230).

As your child becomes more familiar with the idea of recognising objects by their shape and feel, you can secretly introduce new objects which he has not seen or is not familiar with. Look for the surprise on his face when he finds strange objects underneath the cloth!

The Treasure Chest – This game requires the skilful use of two hands (see *Skilful Play*, p. 124).

The basic idea is for your child to open a box to obtain a reward – a favourite toy, or a sweet. But this box is rather special. It has a lot of different fastenings on it. In Fig. 48 we show a box with four types of fasteners – a sliding bolt, a hasp and staple, a toggle and a press-stud (on strips of material).

You can, in fact, use any number of fastenings. The important thing is that they should be as varied as possible, so that your child has to work out the different ways they undo. The box should be strong enough to take all these fastenings (plywood will be ideal).

If you make it big enough your child can use it as a special store box to keep his favourite toys in. But remember this box next time the cat goes missing!

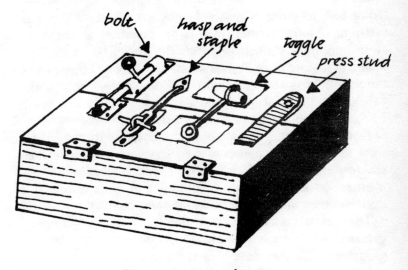

Treasure chest

Fig. 48

BOOKLET 2: LIKE AND UNLIKE

To be able to group together a collection of seemingly quite different objects, because they have something in common, is an important skill. It demands the ability to 'abstract' a common feature from objects which may usually appear quite unrelated. It is this 'abstracting' skill which leads to the development of concepts – and as we have said before, much of our adult thinking is based on concepts.

However, the beginnings of such conceptual thinking are to be found in the activities of even very young children when they match one object with another, either because they are identical or because they are both alike in some respect (for example, they might both be of the same colour).

These early matching games then lead on into 'grouping' games in which the young child sorts objects into particular groups because they have something in common.

In this booklet we have suggested various games which will encourage your child to develop these important ways of thinking about the world around him. In the first part of the booklet we describe a variety of simple matching games, which naturally lead into the 'sorting' games in the latter part of the booklet. So, while you should glance quickly through the whole booklet, it is most likely that you will want to start on the early matching games before progressing to the sorting games.

Matching Games

Colour Dominoes – Colour Dominoes is a matching game in which your child learns to match identical colours. The game is played exactly like ordinary dominoes except, of course, that the dominoes have colours rather than numbers of dots.

You can make your own set of colour dominoes very easily, by painting some small pieces of plywood in two colours. Before you try to teach your child to play colour dominoes, give him plenty of opportunities simply to handle the dominoes and to see what different colours they are.

Your child will most easily learn the rules of Colour Dominoes by watching you play it with other people.

If he shows an interest in the game (and if he doesn't, then don't force him), you can gradually involve him in playing your dominoes for you:

1. Allow him to place a domino in the correct position (i.e. so that identical colours lie side by side) and emphasise, by pointing, that the colours are identical.

2. Allow him to choose the correct domino by himself. If he chooses incorrectly, then he obviously hasn't fully learned the game. Allow him to make further choices until he is correct. Again, emphasise that the colours are identical when the domino is set in place.

3. When you are confident that he has grasped the rules of the game you may wish to drop out altogether. However, this could create a problem – does he know what to do when he can't go, when one usually says 'pass'? This part of the game is not related to his matching skills so you may not wish to teach him the rule at this stage. In this case it would be better to stay with him for the time being. But, to give him the confidence in making his own decisions, why not 'play dumb' and make some wrong choices, so that he can correct you?

Picture Dominoes – When your child has mastered the Colour Dominoes game you can move onto Picture Dominoes. In fact, you can buy sets of picture dominoes in many toy shops. Play Picture Dominoes exactly as you played Colour Dominoes, going through the game stage by stage. You will probably find, though, that you can pass through the early stages fairly quickly, as your child will have grasped the idea of the game by playing Colour Dominoes.

Snap – Do you remember, as a child, all the fun and excitement in playing 'Snap' with your family and friends? Snap is an ideal matching game for your child as it is very lively and the rules are fairly simple.

Packs of Snap cards can be bought at most toy shops. Alternatively, you can make a much easier pack of cards, by simply using different colours. Thus the matching task is very similar to Colour Dominoes. If your child finds the colours rather easy, you can use pictures of objects stuck onto plain postcards (*Early Language Stamps* sold by LDA are gummed sheets of pictures of everyday objects, e.g. balls, shoes, chairs, etc). Have at least two pictures of each object in your pack.

In order to win, of course, you have to be the first to say 'Snap!' If your child is not yet using language, then you could introduce another action, such as clap hands. (Of course, looking in the other direction, snap could also be a very useful way of encouraging your child to start vocalising.)

This is a good game because he will easily understand that he is the winner when he has got all the cards.

Picture Bingo – You can buy games of picture bingo or lotto in many toyshops. This game is usually played with three or four players, so it encourages social play as well as being a matching game.

The rules are quite simple. One player acts as the 'caller' while each other player has a board in front of him, divided into squares. In each square is a picture of an object or an animal.

The 'Caller' then turns up, one at a time, cards with identical pictures to those on the board. Each player can claim pictures that match those on his board. The first one to cover his board with matching picture cards is the winner.

When playing this game with your child you may wish to use only a few pictures at first. So take away the extra cards from the pack and cover the extra squares on each board. Alternatively, you can make your own miniature picture bingo set using the same pictures as in 'Snap' above.

Matching Shapes – Many toy shops sell very attractive 'posting boxes' into which your child can post objects of different shapes – triangles, squares, circles etc. However, these posting boxes may at first be too complicated for your child as they have so many different shapes and holes. You may need to build up your child's understanding of shape very gradually.

Here are some ideas:

Formboards – These are a very handy way of encouraging your child's interest in the shape of objects. At first, your child may only be able to take the shapes out of the board. This is a start and you should encourage it. If your formboard has interesting pictures beneath each shape so much the better, for you can invent a little story to tell as the pictures are uncovered.

Your child may well be more interested in the pictures and the story than in the shape of the covers. This doesn't matter, because if he wants the story told again, he has to put all the shapes back again. You may have to help him, with physical prompts, to put the shapes back, as some are much more difficult than others. Circular shapes are the easiest because you do not have to worry which way up they are, as you do with squares and triangles.

If you are handy with a fretsaw, then you can easily make your own formboard out of plywood, with a cardboard backing. Now you can tailor the shapes to your own requirements, perhaps starting with a board with only circular shapes to give your child plenty of initial practice. Later you can introduce formboards with more difficult shapes.

Do not worry if the pieces in your formboard do not fit as snugly as commercially made ones. In fact, for a child who may have difficulty in controlling his hand movements it will be better if the pieces only fit loosely, but slot more easily into the board.

Home-made Posting Boxes – As we have said, shop-bought posting boxes may have too many holes and shapes for your

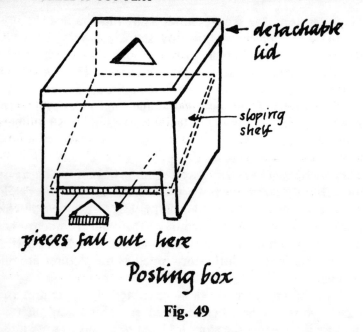

detachable lid

sloping shelf

pieces fall out here

Posting box

Fig. 49

child to cope with at first. You can solve this problem by making your own posting box – as we show in Fig. 49.

This posting box has a detachable top with just one hole in it. The advantage of this posting box is that your child can learn about different shapes one at a time. Have a variety of tops, each with a different shaped hole. You can make, or buy, matching objects to be posted through the hole.

The secret of this game, though, is how much fun you can make it. Just posting objects may not be very interesting for your child (but each child is different so we can't make general rules). So, in our posting box we have put a ramp in the bottom. Now, as each object is posted, it shoots out at the bottom!

When your child has learned about the shapes one at a time, you can then introduce tops with two different shaped holes. Now, of course, he can post two objects at a time and watch them both flying out together!

When your child is capable of posting three or four different shapes he will have become quite skilled in shape-matching. Now you can buy him a toy shop posting box to play with. In addition, remember that you can also play other games, like Dominoes, Snap, Twins etc., using shape as the basis for matching.

All Creatures Great and Small – This is a matching game in which your child matches pictures of fully-grown animals with their offspring – such as a hen with a chick or a cow with a calf. Unless you can draw these yourself, you will have to be quite resourceful to build up a collection of these pictures. So look out for suitable pictures to cut out from magazines or to trace from books. Alternatively, you could ask the local vet if he has any old charts or pictures.

The idea is to stick a picture of the adult animal onto a card. Then cut off a piece of that card. On this piece you stick the picture of the baby animal. We give an example, in Fig. 50,

All creatures great and small

Fig. 50

of a cat and a kitten. The object is to match the kitten with the cat by fitting the small card onto the big card.

Set the big cards out in front of your child and give him the little cards, all mixed up. He now has to match each little animal with the big ones in front of him.

As usual, start with just one or two animal pairs to show your child how to play the game. To help him, cut a different shape off each card for the little animal. This will make it easier for him to match the cards correctly.

Twins – 'Snap' or 'Picture Bingo' may not be appropriate for the child who finds social situations difficult or who is slow in responding. 'Twins' is an alternative matching game which allows the child to work out his solutions at his own speed.

You can use the same cards for 'Twins' as you do for 'Snap'. At first, use only two pairs of cards. Then gradually increase the number as your child gets better at the game. Spread all the cards face-down in front of your child. Now lift *one* of the cards and hold it up to your child. He has to turn over the other cards one at a time until he has found the twin to your card. You could allow him to 'post' the twins in a box, or simply keep them by his side. Then you could turn up a new card and ask him to find the twin again.

Initially, you may have to show him how to play the game by modelling the procedure for him. When he starts to turn the cards over it may be helpful to leave the wrong cards face-up until he has found the twin. However, as he gets better at the game, you can increase the challenge by always turning the wrong cards face down again.

One and One Make One! – It may take you some time to build up your collection of animal pictures for 'All Creatures Great and Small'. In the meantime, here is a simpler matching game which is very easy to make.

All you need are pictures of people or objects (magazines and catalogues are full of them) and a good supply of thin board. Offcuts of plywood will be ideal here, so ask your local hardware shop to keep the spare pieces for you.

Stick each picture on a separate piece of board and then cut it into two further pieces. Keep one piece of each picture and give the other piece to your child. Then set out all your pieces in front of him. Now, of course, he has to match each of his pieces with the right one in front of him. He will probably find it both funny and surprising to see how two 'nonsense' shapes fit to make a proper picture!

As he gets better at the game you can make it harder by cutting each piece in half again. Now he has to fit four pieces together to make the picture. This will be pretty difficult at first so take him through it very slowly, using one picture at a time.

When he can eventually sort a jumble of sixteen pieces into one picture you will know that his sorting and matching skills have developed considerably. You may also think that he is well on the way to doing jig-saw puzzles. You're absolutely right! But steady now, let's take him through the stages gradually. There are two things to bear in mind:

1. Jig-saw puzzles can have as many pieces as you can imagine. But so far, your child may only be able to combine four pieces. So the next step for him would be to make a picture from, say, six pieces. Certainly no more than eight. As he gets better, you can gradually increase the number of pieces.
2. Jig-saw puzzles are usually made up of 'curly' rather than straight-edged pieces. These curly edges may be quite difficult for your child to match, so start him off on a two-piece curly-edged picture. Then, as before, you can go onto more difficult 4-piece and 8-piece pictures.

Who made that sound? – Now for some extra fun!

The object of this game is to match animals with the sounds that they usually make. The funny part is, of course, that *you* have to make the sounds – so start practising those oink-oinks and quack-quacks!

A set of toy farm animals will be ideal for this game – or you could draw pictures of animals on postcards.

At first, you will have to introduce your child to all the

different animal noises. So take each animal in turn and spend some time showing your child the noise it makes, until he has become used to all the animal noises.

Now set out all the animals in front of your child and encourage him to hand you one. Each time he does so you have to make the right noise. This will further help him to match the noise with the animal.

Later on you can make the noise first and then get him to choose the correct animal in front of him. This will tell you how well he has matched each noise with the right animal. Alternatively, if your child is making the animal noises himself, you can hold animals up for him to match the right noise.

As you can imagine, this game can be very funny, so enjoy yourself. There's no reason why thinking shouldn't be fun as well.

This last game involves the skill of matching what something looks like with the noise that it makes. We have already suggested how you can match what an object looks like with what it feels like ('Lucky Dip', p. 227). You can devise other games which will help your child to match what an object tastes like, or smells like, with what it looks like. For example, you could blindfold your child and hold an orange up for him to smell or taste. If he is using language, then you can ask him what it was. If not, take his blindfold away and see if he can choose the orange from a group of different foods.

Hunt the Thimble – In the previous game we showed you how you could turn it into a memory game by turning all the wrong cards face down again. 'Hunt the Thimble' is another memory game.

The idea of this game is to remember where an object has been left, or hidden. As an easy version of the game use two small objects – say a marble and (why not?) a thimble. Hide them each one under a separate cover (a cup, a handkerchief or a cushion) in front of your child. Then get him to find the marble, for example, either by telling him or by showing him another marble.

This game is very easy, of course, but you can quickly make it harder in two ways. First, you can increase the time interval between hiding the object and letting your child find it. Second, you can increase the number of objects and the number of hiding places.

At first you could have three cups instead of two. Then, if your child can move around, you can enlarge the 'hiding area' to the whole room or even the whole house and garden. Of course, you must always show your child where you have hidden the objects otherwise he can't use his memory but has to rely on guesswork.

Sorting Games
When we, as adults, engage in some sorting activity, we usually have a clear rule in mind. For example, sorting out the family wash, we may put the whites on one side and all the coloured garments on the other. The objects in each pile have some specific quality or property in common – in this case white or coloured.

This type of sorting – according to some particular common property – develops out of the much simpler sorting games of young children. Young children start off by grouping things together for reasons which we cannot always understand. They may make two 'piles' or 'heaps' of objects simply so that the heaps are roughly the same shape or size. The objects in each 'heap' appear quite unrelated. Or they may put a red brick with a red ball because they are both red – then add a green shoe – ''cos red and green are nice', then add a piece of string ''cos it's the lace for the shoe'.

This may not be sorting as we understand it but it is the forerunner to later, more logical sorting activities. So when you find your child making such 'piles' with the toys from his rummage box, don't try to get him to do it 'the right way'. Rather, encourage him to sort as he wants to. He is, after all, working out his own rules (even if they keep changing!) and this is all very necessary experience for later sorting games. He is grasping the idea of sorting – the idea that the world isn't just full of different things but that some of them go together.

However, when your child has had a lot of practice in these first sorting games, you may wish to encourage him to make his sorting activity more ordered and systematic. Here are some ideas:

Sort 'em Out – Perhaps the simplest kind of sorting game is to sort, into two groups, objects which look very different from each other. Take, for example, wooden beads versus bottle-tops.

Place two containers in front of your child (preferably transparent ones, like glasses or jam jars) so that he can see what's inside. The game is to sort the beads into one container and the bottle-tops into the other.

Initially, you may need to demonstrate the game by putting some beads into one container and some bottle-tops into the other. However, it is best to let your child have a go as soon as possible.

At first, give him the beads and bottle-tops one at a time, for if you give him a pile of objects he may be more interested in playing with the pile than in sorting the individual objects. Every time he correctly 'sorts' an object, give him plenty of praise. If, however, he places the object in the wrong container just take it out and place it in front of him again. As before, praise him when he gets it right.

When all the objects have been sorted, he may find it a special treat to tip all the objects out of the containers. So let him! After all, he's earned it. But what is more, you can get him to really mix them up – just right for sorting again.

Remember though, that novelty is the keynote with puzzle games. So, in order to maintain your child's interest, you've got to ring the changes. Here are some ideas:

1. *Change the objects* – Instead of the beads and the bottle-tops, for example, you could use marbles and 2p coins. Any small objects which you can obtain easily will be suitable for these sorting games.

2. *Increase the number of groups* – The greater the number of groups to be sorted, the more interesting the game is. When your child has got the idea of sorting into two groups, add a third container and a third set of objects, and so on.

3. *Using an implement* – Instead of sorting by hand, get your child to use a spoon and fork, or a pair of sugar tongs to lift the objects. This will provide him with a new challenge in the game.

4. *Speed sorting* – You can add excitement to the game by encouraging your child to sort the objects as fast as possible. As soon as he has correctly sorted one object, place another one in front of him and urge him to be as quick as possible. *Provided they are capable of the task*, children take great delight in these fast activities, so join in the fun yourself.

When your child has grasped the idea of sorting you can gradually increase the difficulty of the sorting task. This will provide a further challenge to his thinking and will help maintain his interest in these types of games. Here are some ideas:

Not Exactly Alike – The previous game did not require your child to 'abstract' the common property of all the objects in one group, because they were alike in *all* respects. They were identical to each other. However, it is this 'abstracting' skill which we wish to encourage and, like other skills, it is developed gradually.

The next step is to get your child to sort objects which, while not identical, are still quite similar. Take the example of the wooden beads and the 2p coins. Both groups can be enlarged to produce similar but not identical objects. The wooden beads could be of different sizes, colours and shapes (oval, round or cylindrical). The 2p coins could be mixed with ½p, 1p, 5p and 10p coins. Of course, if we consider the coins not just as coins but as circular flat objects, then we could add tiddleywinks counters as well.

As you can see, your child can no longer group the objects because they are identical, but he will have to work out what is the common feature in each group.

Happy Families – This game, which you will remember from childhood days, follows on from the previous game and it also follows on from 'All Creatures Great and Small' (p. 235).

You can buy very attractive packs of 'Happy Families' cards in most toy shops. As you will understand the idea of this game we will not repeat it here.

However, your child may find the rules of the game quite tricky. It is very hard to grasp the notion of which cards are worth keeping and which cards are worth throwing away. So we suggest you invent rules to suit your own child. Here is a possible example:

1. As with 'Colour Dominoes', p. 230, you should partner your child to guide him through the game.
2. All players (usually there are three or four) lay their cards face up so that everyone can see them.
3. Each player, in turn, can choose a card from someone else in exchange for one of his own cards.
4. Of course, this game could end up with everyone stopping everyone else making a family of four cards. So, somebody has to be charitable and not mind losing. Alternatively, you can make the rule that once any player has three cards of a kind, then they can refuse to exchange these cards when asked to.

Picture Sorting – As your child develops his sorting skills you will want to widen the range of objects for him to sort. Obviously, it makes sense to use things with which your child is reasonably familiar. But here you have a problem. Some of these things may not be very suitable for sorting. If you wanted your child to sort trees and birds, for example, the problems are quite apparent.

The solution is, of course, to use pictures. Your first picture-sorting games can be quite simple. Two groups with identical objects in each group – say red cars and yellow balls.

But be ready to move on quickly to more difficult, and more interesting games, otherwise your child will soon get bored. Building on the previous game, you could have cars of different colours and shapes, long and short, large and small, and balls of different sizes, colours and patterns – some with stripes and some with dots.

As with the previous sorting games, don't forget to ring the changes as we suggested on p. 240.

Picture Dominoes – This is a variation of a picture-sorting game. We have already described Colour Dominoes and Picture Dominoes earlier on pp. 230 & 231). In those games the idea was to match identical dominoes – either identical colours or identical pictures.

Now you can have a more difficult picture dominoes game by using pictures of different *types* of objects. You could, for example, use pictures of a football, a tennis ball, a cricket ball. They are all different in various ways but they are all the same in one respect – they are each a *type of ball.*

You can apply the same rule to many other kinds of pictures. You can have pictures of different kinds of shoes, of cars, of foods.

When your child can match *types* of objects successfully, you will know that he is well on the way to thinking in terms of concepts rather than specific objects.

So far your child has been sorting pictures of different *types* of objects. Another kind of sorting activity is to sort pictures by physical qualities like colour and shape.

Colour Sorting – By now you will have a collection of pictures of various objects with different colours. Now, instead of putting all the cars and the balls and the shoes and the houses etc. into their respective groups your child has to sort all the red ones, for example, into one group and all the green ones into another.

In order to succeed in this game your child will have to change his way of thinking about the pictures which he originally sorted into types of objects.

Shape Sorting – You will need to make some fresh cards for this game. On each card draw a distinct shape – a circle, a square, a star, a crescent moon, a cross, a triangle. Have about six cards of each shape, each in a different colour.

At first, play the game with only two shapes, for example

the circle and the cross. Then gradually introduce new shapes as your child gets the idea.

To add a further challenge to the game you may wish to draw your shapes in different colours.

It is very likely that your child will sort the cards by colour at first, and will pay no attention to the shapes. If he does, do not prompt him to the correct solution. He has to work this out for himself. As before, whenever he incorrectly sorts a card just put it back in front of him.

Odd Man Out – This is a reversal of the idea of sorting and matching. Instead of finding the objects that are alike, your child has to choose the one that's different.

You can play 'Odd Man Out' as a variation on many of the sorting games which we have described in this booklet. But remember to keep the materials in this game at the same level as those in the sorting game. If your child is sorting by colour alone, then play 'Odd Man Out' with colours, and so on.

You will need at least three objects, or pictures. Two of these should be the same, while the third is the odd man out. Let us say that you had two red objects, or pictures, and one blue one. If your child understands language, then you can ask him for the one that is 'not red'. If he does not understand language, then you can place a box or tray in front of him. When he places the 'odd man out' in the box, give him a reward – perhaps a small chip of chocolate. If he places the wrong one in the box, simply take it out and replace it in front of him. Let him try again until he chooses the right one.

Every time your child is successful, you should take away the objects and introduce fresh ones – two yellow ones and a green one for example. At first his choices will be based on 'trial-and-error' until he has worked out the rule of the game. But, with sufficient practice, he will come to understand the notion of 'odd man out'.

What's the Use? – This game adds variety to your child's sorting activities because it requires that objects be grouped together, not because they look in some way alike, but because they are used in similar ways.

Let's start with a very simple version of this game:

1. Place two large sheets of paper or cardboard on either side of your child.

2. Think of two types of objects which your child uses in very different ways – for example food and clothing. Now get three kinds of food – say an apple, a carrot and a piece of bread; and three items of clothing – a sock, a scarf and a glove.

3. These objects are to be sorted into separate groups – one group on each sheet of paper. Give your child the idea of the game by sorting the objects yourself at first. Then give him the objects one by one to sort himself. If he gets it right, give him plenty of praise initially. But as the game goes on you will probably find that he derives most satisfaction from simply playing the game. Whenever he makes a mistake, just replace the object in front of him so that he can choose again.

This game can be expanded in two ways:

(a) You can add more objects to each of the groups that he now sorts. Thus you can add an onion or a biscuit to the food and a hat and a shirt to the clothing.

(b) You can replace or add to the original groups with new types of objects, like eating implements or furniture (doll's house size!).

If your child is able to recognise pictures of objects then you can make the game more fun by sticking the 'sorting' sheets on the wall. He can then stick the pictures onto the sheets with a little tab of masking tape (very easy to stick, but also very easy to remove for re-sorting).

Collecting – Following on from the last game, your child can use the wall-sheets for collecting pictures of objects, or even the objects themselves if they are light enough. Young children love to build up their own collections of all sorts of things. This is well worth encouraging because again it is a classifying activity.

Magazines and catalogues are full of pictures of people and objects which your child may like to cut out and stick on his wall-sheet.

When you are out in the park, keep an eye open for different kinds of leaves to bring home (and keep the other eye open for the park-keeper!).

If you are on good terms with your local barman or barmaid (who's blushing now?) why not ask them to save different beer-mats and bottle tops for you?

These are some of the early collecting activities which are the fore-runners of the child's later interest in hobbies like collecting stamps, train-numbers etc.

SOME MORE BOOKS ON PLAY

ATACK, S. M. *Art Activities for the Handicapped* (Souvenir Press, London, 1980)

CASTON, D. *Easy to Make Toys for Your Handicapped Child* (Souvenir Press, London, 1983)

JEFFREE, D. M. *Let Me Count* (Souvenir Press, London, 1989)

JEFFREE, D. & MCCONKEY, R. *Let Me Speak* (Souvenir Press, London, 1976)

JEFFREE, D. & CHESELDINE, S. *Let's Join In* (Souvenir Press, London, 1984)

LEAR, R. *Play Helps* (Heinemann, London, 1977)

MCCONKEY, R. & JEFFREE, D. *Let's Make Toys* (Souvenir Press, London, 1981)

NEWSON, J. & NEWSON, E. *Toys and Playthings* (Penguin, Harmondsworth, 1979)

RIDDICK, B. *Toys and Play for the Handicapped Child* (Croom Helm, London, 1982)

USEFUL ADDRESSES

(i) Toy and Book Suppliers

Many of the following firms will send their catalogues on request:

John Adams Trading Co. Ltd., The Lodge, Crazies Hill, Wargrave, Berks. RG10 8LY. Tel: (073 522) 3480.

E. J. Arnold & Son, Parkside Lane, Dewsbury Road, Leeds LS11 5TD. Tel: (0532) 772112.

Early Learning Centre, Hawksworth, Swindon, Wiltshire SN2 1TT.

Escor Toys Ltd., Groveley Road, Christchurch, Hants. BH23 3RQ. Tel: (0202) 485834.

Fisher-Price Toys, Lodge Farm Industrial Estate, Hopping Hill, Northampton NN5 7AW.

543 Educational Games, 8 Westgate, Tranmere Park, Guiseley, Leeds LS20 8HL. Tel: (0943) 77945.

Four to Eight, Medway House, St Mary's Mills, Evelyn Drive, Leicester LE3 2BT.

James Galt & Co. Ltd., Brookfield Road, Cheadle, Cheshire SK8 2PN. Tel: (061 428) 8511.

Hamleys of Regent Street Ltd., 188 Regent Street, London W1R 6BT. Tel: (01) 734 3161.

Hestair Kiddicraft Ltd., Park Avenue, Aztec West, Almondsbury, Bristol BS12 4RF. Tel: (0454) 616005.

Ladybird Books Ltd., PO Box 12, Beechers Road, Loughborough, Leics. LE11 2NQ. Tel: (0509) 268021.

LDA/Living and Learning, Duke Street, Wisbech, Cambs. PE13 2AE. Tel: (0945) 63441.

Mothercare (UK) Ltd., Cherry Tree Road, Watford, Herts. WD2 5SH. Tel: (0923) 33577.

Orchard Toys, Formlend Ltd., Debdale Lane, Keyworth, Nottingham NG12 5HN. Tel: (0607) 73547.

Philip & Tacey Ltd., Walworth Industrial Estate, Northway, Andover, Hants. SP10 5BA. Tel: (0264) 61171.

Sophia Ltd., Woodpecker Toys, Ivydene Lane, Ashurst Wood, West Sussex RH19 3TN. Tel: (0342) 314033.

Tridias Ltd., 124 Walcot Street, Bath BA1 5BG. Tel: (0225) 64970.

Tupperware, Tupperware House, 130 College Road, Harrow, Middx. HA1 1BQ. Tel: (01) 861 1819.

The Winslow Press Ltd., 23 Horn Street, Winslow, Buckingham, Bucks. MK 18 3AP. Tel: (029 671) 3776.

(ii) Organisations

The following organisations can often provide information about special equipment or details of local branches:

AFASIC (Association for All Speech-Impaired Children), 347 Central Markets, Smithfield, London EC1A 9NH (01-236 6487).

Association for Spina Bifida and Hydrocephalus (ASBAH), 22 Upper Woburn Place, London WC1H 0EP (01-388 1382/5).

British Epilepsy Association, Anstey House, 40 Hanover Square, Leeds LS3 1BE (0532 621076).

British Institute of Mental Handicap, Information and Resource Centre, Wolverhampton Road, Kidderminster, Worcs DY10 3PP (0562 850251).

Committee for Rudolph Steiner Special Education, Educational Registrar, St Christopher's School, 2 Carisbrooke Lodge, Westbury Park, Bristol BS6 7JE (0272 736875/733301).

Disabled Living Foundation, 380 Harrow Road, Paddington, London W9 2HU (01-289 6111).

Down's Syndrome Association, 12–13 Clapham Common Southside, London SW4 7AA (01-720 0008).

Invalid Children's Aid Association, 126 Buckingham Palace Road, London SW1W 9SB (01-730 9891).

Kith & Kids, c/o Thomas Coram Foundation, 40 Brunswick Square, London E1 5AW (01-377 0314).

MENCAP (Royal Society for Mentally Handicapped Children and Adults), 123 Golden Lane, London EC1Y 0RT (01-253 9433).

National Autistic Society, 276 Willesden Lane, London NW2 5RB (01-451 3844).

National Children's Bureau, 8 Wakley Street, London EC1V 7QE (01-278 9441).

National Federation of Gateway Clubs, Gateway Headquarters, 117 Golden Lane, London EC1Y 0RT (01-253 9433).

Opportunity Groups for Pre-School Handicapped Children, Adviser for Special Needs, Pre-School Playgroups Association, 61–3 Kings Cross Road, London WC1 (01-833 0991).

PLAY MATTERS/The Toy Libraries Association for Handicapped Children, 68 Churchway, London NW1 1LT (01-387 9592).

Royal National Institute for the Blind, 224 Great Portland Street, London W1N 6AA (01-388 1266).

Royal National Institute for the Deaf, 105 Gower Street, London WC1E 6AH (01-387 8033).

Scottish Council on Disability, Information Department, Princes House, 5 Shandwick Place, Edinburgh EH2 4RG (031 229 8632).

Scottish Society for the Mentally Handicapped, 13 Elmbank Street, Glasgow G2 4QA (041 226 4541).

SENSE (National Deaf-Blind and Rubella Association), 311 Gray's Inn Road, London WC1X 8PT (01-278 1000).

The Spastics Society, 12 Park Crescent, London W1N 4EQ (01-636 5020).

Voluntary Council for Handicapped Children, c/o National Children's Bureau, 8 Wakley Street, London EC1V 7QE (01-278 9441).

INDEX OF GAMES

INDEX OF GAMES